Christian Men Who Hate Women

BOOKS IN THE **LIFELINES FOR RECOVERY**
SERIES

Zondervan's **Lifelines for Recovery** series emphasizes
healthy, step-by-step approaches for dealing with specific
critical issues.

LIFELINES FOR RECOVERY

Christian Men Who Hate Women

Healing Hurting Relationships

Dr. Margaret J. Rinck

PYRANEE
BOOKS

Zondervan Publishing House
Grand Rapids, Michigan

Christian Men Who Hate Women
Copyright © 1990 by Margaret Josephson Rinck

This is a Pyranee Book
Published by the Zondervan Publishing House
1415 Lake Drive, S.E., Grand Rapids, Michigan 49506

Library of Congress Cataloging-in-Publication Data

Rinck, Margaret Josephson.
    Christian men who hate women / Margaret Josephson Rinck.
       p. cm.
    Includes bibliographical references.
    ISBN 0-310-51751-6
    1. Abused wives—Pastoral counseling of. 2. Misogyny. I. Title.
BV4596.A2R55   1990
248.8'42–dc20   89–48608
                                                        CIP

Edited by Nia Jones

Designed by Kim Koning

Printed in the United States of America

90 91 92 93 94 95 / LP / 10 9 8 7 6 5 4 3 2 1

This book is dedicated to
the glory of God and
to the memory of my grandparents:
Romilda and Louis Forbes,
Gunnar and Anna Josephson.

CONTENTS

ACKNOWLEDGMENTS

Special thanks to these people who contributed to *Christian Men Who Hate Women: Healing Hurting Relationships*:

Nia A. Jones, our editor, who believed in this book from the moment she saw the manuscript, and Sandra Vander Zicht, our editor, who helped take the book to completion. Both provided courteous and efficient assistance as we passed through the many hurdles of a demanding writing and publishing schedule.

Faith Bonniwell, who assisted with typing and careful proofreading.

Dave and Charlotte Johnston, who typed portions of the manuscript.

Reverend Dave Carder of First Evangelical Free Church, Fullerton, California, who read the proofs and provided helpful suggestions.

Drs. Ruby and Walter Deloss Friesen of Beaverton Family Counseling Center, Beaverton, Oregon, who read the proofs and provided insightful suggestions.

John Carl Rinck, my husband, who provided extensive research, editorial, and design assistance on the book—a result of a close collaborative effort between us.

Friends and clients, who are unnamed but who graciously agreed to have their thoughts, feelings, and experiences shared in this book.

PREFACE

This is a book about a tender and painful subject—hurting relationships—in Christian marriage, more specifically the kind of marriage in which Christian women love men who hate them. People ask why I have written this book. Some (men) in my workshops have speculated as to whether I hate men; why else would I write about this topic in such detail? They apparently assume that exposing this issue to scrutiny implies a dislike or disdain for the male gender. Other people wonder whether I have written from personal experience: "Is her father or husband a misogynist (a man who hates women)?" According to these assumptions, this book is either a way of avenging myself or a therapeutic working out of difficult personal issues.

Let me state clearly: I do not hate men and I never have! In fact I was startled when one male associate asked me how I kept from hating misogynistic men in therapy. It has never occurred to me to hate misogynists because I know the terrible pain that these men carry within themselves, underneath the exterior bravado. At times I do feel anger and indignation about misogynistic behavior, whether it is directed toward wives or myself, but I always remember their inner pain. Underneath all the meanness and charm, these men are lonely, isolated, hurt, confused, and terrified of abandonment. Like the playground bully, misogynists are

11

looking for a way to connect with others; however, the difficulty lies with how they develop relationships. Unfortunately, their unhealthy relational skills wreak havoc for themselves and for their marriages.

Writing about this problem does not require that I write from my own personal experience. I am fortunate and blessed with a loving father and a wonderful husband. It is perhaps my father's love and kindness that enables me to feel and extend the hope of loving male-female relationships to those I counsel and teach. My dad has always honored and deeply respected my mother; I am blessed with a husband who treats me the same way.

No matter what our speculations are when we see misogyny addressed, it is not easy to discuss, especially for those of us within the Christian community. Many of us are bound by the myth that "Christians don't have serious problems"; we feel ashamed to admit to these kinds of problems, so we tend to assign blame. Although it outwardly appears that the misogynist is the "bad guy" in the relationship, in reality he is in *no less pain than the woman, but he usually does not know it.*

Both the man and woman in a misogynistic relationship have learned early in life to respond to pain with different defense mechanisms. The misogynist bullies and manipulates; the woman cries and capitulates. These are deeply established patterns of relating and coping. Such learned behaviors are not easily unlearned; however, change is possible with enough patience, grace, and love from Christian friends, pastors, and therapists.

I've been asked whether I ever see a reverse pattern of discrimination—where the woman hates the man. Sometimes I do, but not as often. I have counseled men and women who have had this kind of a relationship. I've discussed this pattern in my workshops and cassette series on *Male and Female Relationships: Discovering Unhealthy Patterns.*

Since the subject of abuse seems to be such a taboo topic in the Christian community, it behooves us all, whether we are professional therapists, pastors, counselors, or concerned Christians, to become aware of our own views regarding abuse. We may need to look within ourselves first if we strongly reject the idea that misogynistic patterns exist in the Christian community. In the section dealing with therapy and treatment, I discuss transference and countertransference issues of which those of us in the pastoring and helping professions need to be aware.

My hope is that we in the Christian church may move beyond our prejudices. We need to set women—and men— free from the terrible bondage that entraps them in patterns of misogynistic behavior and relationships.

God bless you as you read this book!

Margaret Josephson Rinck, Ed.D.
Cincinnati, Ohio
January 1990

While the publisher recognizes and believes in the equality of the sexes in all aspects, in the interest of easy readability, we have elected to standardize the use of the generic male pronoun. Until our language offers a less awkward circumlocution than "his and/or hers," please understand that there is no offense nor approbation intended by this grammatical convention.

INTRODUCTION

In the movie *My Fair Lady* based on George Bernard Shaw's *Pygmalion,* the erudite Professor Higgins takes Eliza Doolittle, a vulnerable, sensitive flower girl, and attempts to transform her into his image of womanhood. He inadvertently falls in love with her in the process. As Eliza begins to make demands on the professor, he finds it difficult to understand and adjust to her needs. In exasperation he asks, "Why can't a woman be more like a man?"

We might chuckle at the implicit sexism in the professor's remark, but his plaintive question mirrors a widely felt sentiment. The "battle of the sexes" is fought daily in our homes, offices, schools, and churches. Women feel mistreated, bewildered, and hurt by male behavior. Men are charged with insensitivity toward women and their needs and run for cover feeling misunderstood and confused.

The roles of women and men in marriage, the workplace, and the church are often very different from the ideal images taught to us in our youth. Real life is rarely as simple or as conflict-free as portrayed on "Father Knows Best" or "The Donna Reed Show." Many Christians come from homes where there was little appropriate modeling of male and female roles in marriage. The seeds sown by our parents blossom into tangled weeds as we emerge from the honeymoon into "real life."

Dr. Susan Forward has electrified the public consciousness with her captivating book *Men Who Hate Women and the Women Who Love Them*. She demonstrates how misogyny is a subtle but prominent feature of the American home. The image of a charming knight—a successful man who sweeps women off their feet—has always been a part of the American dream. Yet, beneath the fascinating exterior of this man lies the shadow of a menacing second persona. Thousands of women discover, to their dismay, that their dream man is actually Dr. Jekyll and Mr. Hyde.

Often, the dark side of the dream man emerges even before the honeymoon is over, as he begins a campaign designed to keep his wife off balance. This is largely unconscious behavior on his part, but nevertheless it is devastating to the relationship. Criticism, subtle or overt, undermines the woman's self-confidence. Any challenge or objection by his wife is met with rage, temper tantrums, or stony silence. The Christian misogynist (yes—there are such people) often uses distortions of scriptural teaching to keep his partner "in her place." Subtly at first, but increasingly he exerts dominance in every area of life. The methods of control include limiting the availability of household funds, insisting that they change friends or churches, demanding that the woman quit work or discontinue her education, and making demeaning sexual allusions in or out of the bedroom. The scriptural teaching of "mutual submission" and love becomes submerged by a patriarchal dominance and a dwarf theology.

The woman often responds to this situation with bewilderment. The Prince Charming she adored before the wedding now behaves like a beast. She hesitates to tell anyone of her problem because she fears that no one would believe her. Outwardly her husband still appears to others as the sensitive, successful, loving man that she thought she had married, so she begins to doubt the validity of her perceptions and blames herself for problems with the relationship. She works harder to please him and obeys his slightest whim—to gain his approval and respect.

In most instances the wife's efforts to win the love and respect of her husband through overcompensating behavior is doomed to failure. The problem is not a failure to choose the correct behaviors to please her husband; the real issue is that he greatly depends on women but actually hates them. Until his dependency needs are resolved, the relationship cannot be firmly established. The reason is that once the woman changes a particular behavior to please him, another behavior becomes the target. The definition of what is pleasing constantly changes, so that she is kept off balance. She begins to doubt her competence, her femininity—even her sanity! Others may respond to her as a bright, caring, loving person, but according to her spouse, within the marital relationship she is none of these things. She simply cannot win with him. Nothing she does ever seems to please him.

As a result, this woman goes to a therapist or her pastor. These professionals, though well-intentioned, often do not understand the dynamics of misogynistic behavior. Worse still, depending on their cultural or theological outlook, they may even perpetuate misogynistic attitudes and behavior patterns. Consequently, the woman receives no help, and the misogynistic husband remains unaware that his own deeply ambivalent dependency issues and unconscious resentment toward women contribute to the problems in their marital relationship.

In order to understand the dilemma of the victimized woman we must understand what misogyny is. You will notice the phrase "hatred of women" is mentioned frequently throughout this book. This phrase is a literal translation of the

Greek word *misogunia: misein* (to hate) and *gune* (women). Most people are familiar with the "gyny" root as it relates to words like gynecologist. Thus the word *misogyny* literally means hatred of women.[1] The word *hate* is shocking and offensive to our sensitivities, particularly if we apply it to what we perceive as "Christian" men or "Christian" doctrines. As we all have been taught, Christian men and husbands are to love their wives and respect women. Paul tells us in Ephesians 5:29, "No man ever hates his own flesh, but nourishes it and cherishes it, as Christ does the church" (RSV). Logically, no man should be a misogynist (hate his own flesh); the concept is an antithesis, especially for Christian men, since this self-hatred contradicts not only self-love, but also Christ's love for the church with which Scripture compares marriage.

Christian Men Who Hate Women—is it really a contradiction in terminology? An exaggeration or a statement of fact? In *Webster's Ninth New Collegiate Dictionary*, the word *hate* is defined as the "intense hostility and aversion usually deriving from fear, anger, or sense of injury; an extreme dislike or antipathy." We usually think of rapists, mass murderers, or violent wife-beaters as examples of men who hate women. Yet there are men who, while not fitting this dramatic category, also have deep within them a hatred for women. Since their weapons are not usually physical, but rather mental and emotional, their hatred is expressed much more subtly. These men are not, as Susan Forward points out in her book *Men Who Hate Women and the Women Who Love Them,* clear-cut sadists. They do not get a perverse pleasure or sexual thrill out of their wife's pain; however, they do engage in some sadistic behaviors. Although they are not strictly narcissists, as we will see later, they do behave similarly to narcissists at times. *True* narcissists look for admiration above all things and tend to move from one unstable relationship to another in search of it. Misogynists (men who hate women) seem to need to control their wives more than they need their affirmation or admiration.[2] Unlike true narcissists, they are usually able to sustain a long-term commitment to a woman. These men act both lovingly and hatefully with equal passion, so the woman is confused by the double messages of their relationship. No wonder she feels like she lives with Dr. Jekyll and Mr. Hyde. A misogynist feels at once threatened by and enraged by his wife's pain.[3] When he beats her badly or emotionally abuses her and she cries or acts hurt or upset, he is inwardly threatened because her pain unconsciously hooks his own pain, which lies buried deep within. Her anguish seems to feed his fury and hatred. It is as if he despises her for her "weakness" in showing pain or feeling hurt.

One of the unique factors that Dr. Forward discovered when exploring this topic was that misogynists focus their cruelty and destructive behavior almost exclusively on their wives. On one hand, they claim to love their wives passionately, yet they *act* in a way that negates the declaration.[4] Thus at church or at the office these men appear debonair, kind, jovial, and charming. Later we will see that these men are difficult to spot unless you talk with those who live with them. This double-life factor is one reason why Christian women find that their friends at church and often their pastors doubt the veracity of what they describe goes on at home.

Christian men who hate women are in some ways even more dangerous and destructive in their relationships than their non-Christian counterparts. Non-Christian misogynists do not have the additional arsenal of church doctrines, God-talk, and the "sanctioning" of male authority, which comes in a Christian marriage. Their wives are not taught from childhood to "submit" to men "no matter what" because it is

"God's will." Thus Christian relationships based on misogyny are much more complicated due to the theological, cultural, and traditional influences that tend to reinforce the misogynist's prejudice against his wife.

How does a Christian woman recognize whether she is in a misogynistic relationship? What are the telltale signs? One of the major purposes of this book is to explore these symptoms in depth. At this point let me sketch them briefly. Dr. Forward devised a list of questions she uses for counseling women.[5] I have adapted her list to my own experience with Christians to create the following ten guidelines.

A woman should examine whether her marriage relationship has most of these characteristics:

1. The man assumes that he has the "God-given" right to control how she lives and behaves. Her needs or thoughts are not even considered.

2. He uses God, the Bible, and church doctrine to support his "right to tell her what to do," and *demands* that she "submit" unquestioningly to his desires, whims, decisions, or plans. There is no sense of mutuality or loving consideration. It is always his way or nothing.

3. She finds that she no longer associates with certain friends, groups, or even family members because of her need to keep him happy. Even though these activities or people are important to her, she finds herself preferring to avoid them in order to "keep the peace."

4. He believes and acts like her opinions, views, feelings, or thoughts have no real value. He may discredit them on general principle or specifically because "she is a woman and easily deceived like Eve was." Or, he may give lip-service to respecting her thoughts, but later

shoot them down one by one because they "are not logical."

5. He acts charming and sweet at church and is well-liked at work, yet at home the family has to "walk on eggs" to prevent setting him off. People who do not see him at home find it hard to believe that she really is suffering emotional abuse. He reinforces this feeling whenever she points out the differences between home and church by saying something such as, "Oh, quit exaggerating. I'm not like that!"

6. When she displeases him and he does not get his way, he yells, threatens, or sulks in angry silence.

7. She feels confused by his behavior because one day he can be loving, kind, charming, and gentle; the next he is cruel and full of rage. The switch seems to come without warning.

8. No matter how much she tries to improve, change, or "grow in the Word," in her relationship with him, she still feels confused, inadequate, guilty, and somehow off balance. She never knows what will set him off next, and no matter how much she prays, he never changes. She almost feels she must be "crazy" and she is sure it is her fault.

9. He acts possessive and jealous, even of her time with the children. He may even try to restrict her normal church activities because "a woman's place is in the home." If other people, especially other men, notice her or talk to her, he becomes very angry or jealous.

10. When anything goes wrong in the home or in their relationship, the problem is always *her*. If she would just be "more submissive" or "be filled with the Spirit" or "obey me like a good Christian wife," everything would be fine. He seems blind to any cruelty or

21

FIGURE 1: THE RINCK MISOGYNY CONTINUUM

UNCONSCIOUS FOUNDATION OF MISOGYNISTIC BEHAVIOR: SHAME AND FEAR OF ABANDONMENT

This produces a pattern of disrespect and hatred toward women. Misogyny lies on a continuum and is manifested at various levels of intensity, in various types of behaviors and attitudes. To one degree or another, all the types (I through IV) of Christian men who hate women use the Bible, church doctrine, and theological arguments to support their right to control women. He demands "submission" to his viewpoint; He discounts his wife's feelings, opinions, and thoughts. He acts charming one moment, then hostile and cruel the next. He frequently points out his wife's faults. He is unable to perceive his own shortcomings in the relationship.

MILD ➡ ➡ ➡ ➡ ➡ ➡ ➡ ➡ ➡ ➡ ➡ ➡ ➡ ➡ ➡ EXTREME

Type I Misogynist	Type II Misogynist	Type III Misogynist	Type IV Misogynist
No physical abuse of his partner. He uses indirect criticism; denies that he is abusive, prot-estations of love when con-fronted with his disrespectful behavior; extremely subtle, may use flattery to keep woman at his side. Uses logic to con-trol situations. Outargues spouse, totally discounts woman's feelings and thoughts. He rarely loses his temper. He always looks as if he is in con-trol, very reasonable. Out of touch with his own feelings.	Includes Type I behaviors plus more overt verbal tactics such as teasing, bullying, belitting, name-calling, obvious criticism, unfa-vorable comparison of partner with other woman. Uses non-verbal tactics such as pouting, the "silent treatment," dirty looks to show displeasure. May demand special attention. May be jealous of wife's attention to children or other relatives. May use temper tantrums to get his own way. Increase in intensity and fre-quency of behaviors over Type I.	Uses any of Type I and Type II behaviors plus the threat of physi-cal, emotional, or sexual abuse. More extreme in controlling so-cial life, religious practices, fi-nances, sexual interactions, and matters of daily living. Increase in intensity and frequency of behaviors over Types I and II.	Uses any of Type I through Type III behaviors plus physical and/ or sexual abuse toward wife and possibly children. Level of in-tensity of abusive behavior is very high and poses a signifi-cant danger to the woman. Abusive style has become a deeply ingrained behavior. More extreme in controlling various areas of family life.

© 1990 Margaret J. Rinck

misbehavior on his part. He actually sees himself as virtuous for "putting up" with a woman like her.

Not all misogynists are violent or physically abusive. In fact, most are not. The one factor that makes misogyny so difficult to identify is that it is usually extremely subtle, not readily observable to those outside the family system. In order to understand better misogynistic behaviors, we have described the Misogyny Continuum in Figure 1. Type I misogynists on the left side of the continuum represent the mildest forms of misogynistic behaviors, while Type IV misogynists represent the most extreme forms of abusive behaviors. Whether extreme or mild, all these misogynistic behaviors are manifestations of what happens when the root cause of shame and fear of abandonment creates more irrational fear and subsequent hostility. Although Type IV misogynists are the most extreme cases of misogyny and incorporate behaviors from the previous three stages, it is not always the case that a man will progress from Stage I to Stage IV. Because of the uniqueness of every male/female relationship, each misogynistic relationship will also be different, yet share common characteristics that make them misogynistic.

Some people react to the idea of misogyny as if it were only an aberration or an extreme of normal behavior. Some cases of misogyny are dramatic and yet even these cases are not as uncommon as people think. As we saw in the Misogyny Continuum, there are other examples of misogynistic behavior that are less extreme yet still typical of misogyny. Sexist attitudes and subtle forms of misogyny are so accepted in our culture that oftentimes we don't recognize them for what they are. Consequently, we operate on the basis of self-defeating beliefs that contribute to dysfunctional roles in male/female relationships.

When a man has hidden hurt and anger against women, it

comes out in sometimes subtle and sometimes overt attitudes of disrespect toward women. In some cultural groups, misogyny is expressed overtly in lewd, rude, and crudely disrespectful language. Whether in the "boys' locker room" or as a part of the machismo of a particular cultural group, women are represented as mere extensions of the male desire for sex and as objects to be controlled. This attitude is expressed more politely by those who suggest that the best place for a woman is "barefoot, pregnant, and in the kitchen." In other cultural groups, the attitude of misogyny comes out in more genteel ways. Some people who are cultured and highly educated consider such phraseology too blatant. Although they may not use such language or voice opinions that imply a disdain for women, their disrespectful attitude emerges in their overt behavior.

Recently, a pastor friend shared with me a particularly difficult counseling situation, which emphasizes the subtlety of misogyny. She received a call from Amy, who was divorced. Her son Ryan had broken his leg so she asked her sister for help. Amy's brother-in-law took Ryan to the doctor, drove Amy and Ryan home, and helped get Ryan and his wheelchair upstairs. Amy brewed coffee and made a snack for Ryan. When her brother-in-law came downstairs, he edged her against the wall and began to undress her. Shocked and frightened, Amy pulled away and told him to leave. Then she called her pastor for counsel. We have all heard about such incidents happening. Unfortunately, I have often heard people say, "She must have asked for it. He was only doing what comes naturally." The fact is that Amy did nothing to invite such a betrayal of trust. Even though her brother-in-law may have never talked derogatorily to her, his behavior certainly evidenced misogynistic characteristics and generally an acceptance of what I call our society's *Misogyny Myth System*.

There are certain myths, or lies, that get bandied about in our society. Although these false beliefs are not true facts about male/female relationships, they are often repeated, sometimes as a form of dark male humor. In moments of stress and of opportunity, what is a myth begins to be acted upon as truth. For example, a common myth is that "a divorced or separated woman is used to getting it (sex)." A man may reason to himself, *Of course she will want it, and it is my duty to supply it. My advances will be welcomed!"* There is danger when some men who believe these myths are with divorced or separated women because they allow their normal inhibitions to fall away and behave in shockingly inappropriate ways. Studies with college-age male students indicate that another widely-believed myth is that when a woman says no to sex, she really means yes, which may suggest one of the reasons why date-rape has become such a problem in recent years.

We have all heard jokes about these myths, and may even have joked ourselves about them, but we don't really think we believe them or that we would act on these ridiculous caricatures—*especially if we are Christians*. Or, would we? Any unchallenged myth has the potential to work upon us in our unguarded moments. What I am suggesting is the need to be aware of the attitudes, the humor, the deprecatory remarks that we have all heard about women and men. We might not *really* believe them, but they may be more powerful in our subconscious than we think, if the opportunity and emotional climate are conducive to misogynistic behavior.

Misogyny, in all its subtlety, can extend far beyond a marital or dating relationship. We have all heard about the many cases of harassment in the workplace and sexism in business and educational settings. Occasionally misogyny not only affects individuals and couples but whole groups of people as well. In December of 1989, a well-publicized incident in Canada caught my attention. With gun in hand, a twenty-year-old man ran into a Canadian university building and screamed that he hated women and wanted the women separated from the men. He then systematically killed these women and methodically stalked the other women throughout the building. His suicide note informed the police that he hated women and blamed women for all his problems. This dramatic Canadian incident gives a frightening sense of what the extreme of misogyny and prejudice is. But everyday acts of misogyny are no less devastating in their own way to the lives of the men and women involved.

For Christians, it's easy to rationalize, and even deny, that a relationship is misogynistic when the behavior manifestations are mild. Consequently, much misogynistic abuse in the church often remains undetected. As a result, well-intentioned pastors and Christian therapists, who have not studied misogyny, misdiagnose marital problems that are presented to them. If as a pastor or counselor you talk with a woman whose relationship has many of the characteristics (listed on pages 20 and 21), then there is misogyny involved.

The purpose of this book is to enable the women in misogynistic marriages as well as counselors, pastors, and others to identify and understand what is going on in these relationships. There are unique factors within a Christian misogynist relationship. Since denial of the problem is the hallmark of such relationships, it is vital that we first understand what these relationships are and how they work. Then we will discuss how to provide care, support, and treatment to the people involved. Both the woman *and* the man are hurting—both need our love and compassion.

INTRODUCTION

The first few chapters discuss the relationships in great detail: how they start, what happens, how both parties contribute to the dysfunction. The latter chapters examine therapeutic treatment and the role of the church in misogynistic relationships. Within this book I use illustrations from the lives of people I have met in my years of practice. All identifying characteristics and names have been changed so as to ensure privacy. However, the situations and experiences are real, and I have attempted to be as accurate as possible without breaking confidentiality.

1

THE DILEMMA OF SUBMISSION AND ABUSE

Mary Dunbar, age thirty-nine, is the daughter of a brilliant but self-centered and rather eccentric medical school professor and his socialite wife. He was uninvolved in the lives of his six children. Mary's mother is an example of an extremely codependent person who is unable to feel or express any negative emotions or stand up for herself. Mary's parents divorced after a twenty-year marriage when her father went through a "mid-life crisis." Her mother remarried an active alcoholic, and is unavailable because of geographical separation and also because of her obsessive desire to please her alcoholic husband. Mary's father lives in a distant city and is of no emotional support, since he cannot focus upon anyone but himself. Mary has two younger sisters who live out of state.

When Mary was a student she received free tuition at the university where her father taught. There she met John

Dunbar (a student in the Honors Program) during her freshman year. Their relationship began as a result of a mutual interest in drugs, but later they developed a friendship. They became sexually intimate when Mary was eighteen years old and John was nineteen.

Soon Mary thought that she was pregnant, and John said that he would marry her. His father threatened to disown him, so John's friends set up a "hippie-style" wedding, complete with drugs and alcohol. Four days prior to the wedding date, Mary found out that she was not pregnant and told John that they could call off the wedding. At that point John threw her against a building and screamed, "We are getting married! My father has disowned me, and my friends have gone to a lot of trouble! You *are* going to marry me!" Mary felt threatened and married John because she believed that she "had to do" what he said. Her mother had never modeled assertive behavior and Mary did not believe that she had a choice. She was frightened by John's violent outburst and fearful of what he might do if she resisted.

After the wedding, John began to demand bizarre sexual encounters. Within a year John started to criticize, mock, and ridicule Mary in every area of their life together. All this increased her fear of John. She was physically afraid of him and terrified of his emotional rejection so she did all that he requested. Her need for affirmation overtook her and she gave in to his demands.

John and Mary became charismatic Christians after four years of marriage. At first Mary thought that this conversion experience would change John's demands, but his perverse requests continued. John also began physically abusing Mary and their eldest child. Yet Mary said nothing of any of this to anyone. John and Mary were the perfect Christian couple to all outsiders. They were actively involved in their church, and seemed healthy and happy. John even became a lay chaplain for a local sports team.

Some years later, they moved to a large city in another part of the country. This was one of a series of eighteen residence changes in their nineteen years of marriage. John seemed to need to keep his wife and family off balance; he never allowed them to live in one place long enough to develop deep relationships or ties in a community.

At one point both John and Mary became involved in a community movement. Mary, in particular, received much media attention and many affirmations on her speaking, writing, and organizational abilities. John, because of his work commitments, was less involved and became very jealous as Mary received more and more recognition.

Mary experienced a change in her self-concept as she received more and more affirmation and recognition from others. She came to realize that she was a dynamic, bright, talented, capable woman. She had become so accustomed to hearing about her failures, supposed stupidity, and worthlessness from her husband that she had lost all sight of her abilities. As Mary became more active, John became extremely jealous and suspicious of her legitimate business interactions with other men. However, Mary never had a single flirtatious thought. She adored her husband and wanted to please him more than anything else.

Despite Mary's added community responsibilities, she still managed their home and fed and clothed their six children (without any emotional or household support from her husband). She kept their home so immaculate that friends often commented that it looked like a page from *House Beautiful* magazine.

John continued to act abusively to his family. He regularly beat their eldest child, particularly if he failed to achieve perfect scores on his school tests. One time he threw the child down the basement stairs and beat him with a stick. This was because he received a ninety-nine percent on a spelling test. John's explanation for this behavior was "spare the rod and spoil the child." He more or less ignored the other five children. When Mary objected to his neglect and inattention toward the children, he would point to biblical passages on "submission" and tell her that she was not behaving like a good Christian wife.

As is typical of women from abusive marriages, Mary, although extremely bright and college-educated, had very low self-esteem. Over the years she had heard mostly negative rhetoric and criticism from her husband. Mary internalized much of this criticism, and consequently her self-esteem and self-confidence steadily declined throughout her marriage. She would relent and comply when her husband asked her to engage in aberrant sexual acts, because this was the one area in which she could seemingly please him. It is ironic that John as well as the pastors and elders of their church community would later accuse Mary of being "rebellious," since codependent women are people pleasers to an extreme degree. The last thing that Mary desired to do was to displease her husband. Thus she allowed herself to be humiliated and degraded, and stood by helplessly whenever her husband physically abused her or their child. She tolerated outrageous emotional and physical abuse believing that she should be submissive to her husband. Her strong desire to avoid John's displeasure kept her quiet for nineteen years, even though her motherly instincts rankled at these abuses.

Finally Mary summoned her courage and fortitude and confided her problems to a well-respected jurist in the community. Upon his advice, she told her pastor about what was happening in the Dunbar household. She then was further traumatized by the fact that her pastor refused to believe her. She was humiliated and embarrassed to have to confess to her pastor that she had been living a lie for nineteen years. The fact that he refused to believe her was horrifying.

Later, John did confess his "sins" in a meeting with the pastor. However, any relief that Mary might have felt was short-lived. For John, as is typical of men who hate and abuse women, blamed his wife for all of their marital problems. He claimed that his wife was "unsubmissive" and that was why he had engaged in abusive acts against his wife and children. Some examples of the alleged "unsubmissive" behavior included the following: Once in a while dinner might not be on the table immediately when he arrived home from work; sometimes the six children would leave their toys on the floor; occasionally the laundry might not be entirely done on a particular day. These criticisms were directed against a woman whose friends could affirm that she kept her home immaculate, despite six children and their unpredictable behavior.

The pastor and elders who met with the Dunbars failed to discern the real issues. The focus of their counseling emphasized Mary's supposed shortcomings. The pastor and elders set up the following list of rules to govern her life.

RULES PLACED ON THE DUNBARS BY THEIR PASTOR AND ELDERS

PREFACE: In order to help establish peace and harmony between Mary and John Dunbar especially while they are receiving counseling; and by God's grace desiring to see Mary and John glorify God in their marriage; and in order to help define specifically what the biblical responsibilities of husbands and wives are; and to help establish positive habits

33

of relating to one another; we propose the following covenant vow between Mary and John Dunbar.

A COVENANT VOW BETWEEN MARY AND JOHN DUNBAR

Acknowledging and confessing our sins before God of not being all that He calls us to be as husband and wife and looking to Jesus Christ as the only one in whom forgiveness and reconciliation is possible and the one who grants His power and strength to build a God-honoring biblical marriage, I do promise and covenant before God and these elders to take the following steps toward reconciliation with my spouse over the next three months:

JOHN:

1. I will not drink any alcoholic beverages whatsoever during this time.

2. I will not threaten my wife about leaving her at all (including discussions of moving to a foreign country, Mary needing to get a job, etc.).

3. I will not go out with Tom. The only time I will spend with him will be at my own home.

4. I will not complain about Mary's housekeeping, appearance, meals, discipline of the children, etc., for the next three months and I will say some positive word to each member of the family daily.

5. I will do the basic chores normally expected of a husband including but not limited to the following:

   a. Make sure cars are clean and in good running order.

   b. Make sure grass is cut/sidewalks cleared of snow/take care of other outdoor responsibilities.

   c. Keep the garage clean and tidy.

   d. Do indoor repairs or see that they are done (I will bring list to my weekly meeting with the pastor showing what I have done).

6. I will meet with an elder weekly for an hour of prayer and study.

7. I will see the psychiatrist weekly for counseling.

8. I will limit my outside activities beyond direct work, home, and church activities to a maximum of five hours per week and will tell the pastor every week how I intend to spend those hours for the following week (i.e., Cub Scouts, etc.).

9. I will lead the family in devotions at least three times per week.

MARY:

1. I will never challenge or defy my husband in front of the children. If we reach a disagreement on a matter, I will call the pastor or an elder to arbitrate.

2. I will attend all church worship services (A.M. and P.M.) with my family with a visible enthusiasm. I will also attend the weekly women's Bible study, the fall women's retreat, and most other church functions (i.e., missions conference, church anniversary picnic, etc.).

3. I will meet weekly with a church fellowship partner for an hour of prayer and study.

4. I will see the psychiatrist weekly for counseling.

5. I will stop all relationship with the following men: (Lists seventeen men, including prominent pastors, community leaders, and neighbors) and "all other men." This includes telephone as well as personal interactions. Casual interaction with these men in church or with John present is acceptable.

6. I will limit my outside activities beyond direct home and church activities to five hours per week and will tell the pastor each week how I intend to spend those five hours. Any of the following activities will count toward the five-hour limit: Political activities, meetings, media events, article and letter writing, speeches, and telephone activity.

7. I will do the following household and family tasks:

a. FOOD—See that the weekly shopping is done.
—Prepare lunches every day.
—Prepare a balanced dinner each night Monday through Saturday between 5:30 and 6:30 P.M. (John prepares main meal on Sundays.)

b. LAUNDRY—Wash one load of laundry each day Monday through Saturday (second load done by oldest daughter) to include gathering, washing, drying, folding, ironing, and putting away.

c. CLEANING—Keep the house picked up daily of diapers/papers/etc., and get the garbage to the kitchen for John to take out to the cans.
—Vacuum Monday and Friday downstairs and weekly upstairs.
—Dust weekly downstairs and every other week upstairs.
—Thoroughly clean bathrooms once each week.
—See that the dishes are done daily before going to bed (with Carol's help).
—See that the children are bathed daily.

—The maid will be dismissed for now. The possibility of rehiring her will be a topic of discussion at the six-week review time. If she is rehired, her duties would be for cleaning except for the toilets and the bathroom, which is to be Mary's responsibility.

8. I will bring a list to my weekly meeting with the church fellowship partner and show the items that I have performed in Point Seven.

I see that I need to spend my major energy and effort over the next three months prayerfully and diligently working to be faithful to the above requirements placed on me by the elders and I submit to the authority and oversight of the elders in these matters. If my spouse does not live up to the requested items above, I will not take the matter up with my spouse but with the pastor and the elders.

My responsibility to keep my part of this pledge does not depend on my spouse keeping his or her agreement to these points. I further understand that if I do not keep this pledge satisfactorily that the next stage would be for the whole Board of Elders to be made aware of my failure and to institute disciplinary action according to the guidelines of the Book of Church Discipline. Performance on this agreement will be reviewed after six weeks.

If this agreement works satisfactorily for the three-month period, changes will then be considered such as adding more hours for outside activities and determining what those activities are to be.

I will seek the Lord's grace to patiently endure and bear with my spouse through the ups and downs of the next three months and will expect to see positive improvement in myself and in my spouse to the glory of Christ.

Signed:

John Dunbar   Elder A
Mary Dunbar   Elder B
Pastor Jones   Elder C

The fact that the focus of these rules was almost entirely upon Mary's alleged shortcomings (the victim), rather than upon her husband's irresponsible behavior (the perpetuator of abuse), further increased Mary's depression.

As a result Mary Dunbar sought treatment from a Christian therapist. The Dunbars had previously seen a psychiatrist who reportedly affirmed to Mary that her husband's behavior was a threat to the children. Mary Dunbar reported to her therapist that despite her anxiety regarding this information and the psychiatrist's concern, he did not have time to treat the children. Despite Mary's anxiety and the psychiatrist's concern, her pastor forbid Mary to seek therapy for the children. But eventually she decided to act against her pastor's counsel and sought help for the children.

Does this scenario seem improbable? Is it fiction? An extreme example? Actually it is a true story. This case *has* happened! Today, Mary suffers from Post Traumatic Stress Disorder, Dysthymic Depression, and codependency as the result of the many years of physical and emotional abuse inflicted upon her and her children by her husband John. The trauma of rejection and emotional abuse by Mary's pastor and church elders seriously exacerbated her already severe condition.

Mary Dunbar sees her therapist on a consistent basis. She has had weekly appointments in individual and/or group therapy contexts. The therapy focuses on a number of areas:
1. *Breaking through her denial about what she has experienced as a victim of physical and emotional abuse.* Women who have been abused often experience an irrational need to excuse

or cover up the abuse. This is the so-called "Stockholm Syndrome," in which the victims identify so completely with the victimizer, that they ignore reality and their own needs. They deny the abuse to themselves and to others for so long that they begin to believe that they deserve it. John consistently told his wife that she was incompetent at *everything*. He repeatedly belittled her before the children to reinforce her sense of inferiority and incompetence. Mary must overcome her own denial and that of the children, who have come to believe that treating women badly is "normal" behavior.

2. *Helping her to elicit memories of the trauma and encouraging her to express the painful emotions she has stored for so long.* It will be some time before Mary is able to become fully, consciously aware of her pain and find ways to appropriately express it. Her present relief, now that she is no longer subjected to abuse on a daily basis, is so great that it is masking her underlying pain. Once things settle into a routine, and she is sure that John will not be able to continue abusing her, the pain will reemerge dramatically.

3. *Helping Mary regain a sense of competence, self-mastery, and self-worth.* Mary is an extremely bright, college-educated woman. She needs to reexperience her own abilities and her natural competencies. For example, as a result of John's demeaning and destructive behavior and attitudes toward his wife, their oldest child was recently shocked to discover that Mary actually knew how to write checks! All of the children have learned from watching their father's behavior that it is perfectly appropriate to treat Mary as an incompetent, stupid woman. This has seriously contributed to the erosion of her self-worth. Mary's involvement in the local community activities began to provide a source of positive feedback about her competencies. It cast some

doubt as to her supposed stupidity, and fortunately led her to seek help.

4. *Working through reactions to serious life events and traumas.* Mary still suffers from anxiety attacks when she hears a car pull into the driveway, or looks at the clock and sees that it is 5:00 or 6:00 P.M. (the time when her husband came home). She must learn to desensitize to these and other stimuli which produce anxiety related to the abuse. There are numerous areas where she has developed trauma reactions. Each of these will require time to heal.

5. *Working through themes of forgiveness toward those who have abused and betrayed her.* In a Christian therapy program, the goal is always to lead a person to a place where forgiveness is possible. In order to achieve this goal, much time and release of emotion is necessary. Thus Mary will be in treatment for some time.

6. *Training Mary in assertiveness skills, so as to reduce the likelihood that she will, in the future, succumb to abuse.* Women who are subjected to physical and emotional violence develop a lifestyle of "learned helplessness." Assertiveness training teaches a person how to lovingly but firmly confront others as necessary.

7. *Develop a codependency recovery program.* Women (and men) who live in dysfunctional contexts often learn obsessive "pleasing" behaviors. They become so obsessed with pleasing other people that they submerge their own identity in those persons, neglect themselves, and lose sight of their own legitimate needs. Recovery from codependency requires that the affected person learn how to establish appropriate, healthy boundaries between herself and others. Through individual and group therapy, Mary, as a codependent, is learning how to identify overly responsible or caretaking behavior patterns. She is also

learning to allow others to suffer their own consequences (so that they are not inappropriately protected or rescued). In addition, she gradually finds herself no longer willing to tolerate or enable destructive, abusive behavior. Most importantly, she is learning to trust in God rather than use compulsive caretaking or people pleasing as a way to feel good about herself.

Mary and her children will require regular long-term therapy. Recovery from emotional and physical abuse is often a lifelong process. The fact that Mary's pastor and church elders were inadvertent supporters of the abuse has added to the trauma. This woman has lost everything she had worked to achieve: *a happy Christian home*. It is ironic that in working to achieve a Christian home, Mary was living a lie. No one can have a happy Christian home when there is denial, abuse by one's spouse, abuse of one's children, and constant fear. It was because Mary desired this goal so much that she tolerated indignities and deceived herself into believing that it was a reality—despite daily proof of her husband's emotional illness. It will take her time to recover from the shock of uncovering this lie. It will be even more difficult for her to cope with this as she tries to feed and clothe six children. Yet Mary is a resilient and strong person. Her therapist believes she can overcome these obstacles, given enough time, support, and therapy.

During the last three years, since studying misogyny in Christian marriage, I have seen this basic pattern of abuse repeatedly, with individual nuances. Frequently, the abused woman turns to Christian friends or a pastor for help, and encounters rejection. They may not believe her story, or they underestimate the gravity of the situation. It's tempting for third parties to assume that a "quick fix and a prayer" will remedy the problem.

Kay Marshall Strom illustrates this point in her book *In the Name of Submission: A Painful Look at Wife Battering:*

> "After my husband beat me severely for the third time in a month, I turned in desperation to my minister," said Pamela. "I wish I hadn't. First, he assured me my husband was not a bad man and meant me no harm. Then he instructed me to be more tolerant, more understanding, and to forgive my husband for beating me, just as Christ forgave those who beat him. I went home determined to do better, but I was greeted at the door by a punch in the face. How much must I tolerate? Does Christ really want me to stay in an abusive relationship?"[1]

Strom's example is very sobering. According to the FBI, one of every two women is beaten at some point during her marriage. Twenty-eight percent are battered at least once a year.[2] The research of Straus, Gelles, and Steinmetz in *Behind Closed Doors* suggests that in some cases religious orientation actually aggravates the situation.[3] Yet physical assault is only the tip to the abuse's iceberg.

The emotional abuse perpetuated by the misogynist (a man who hates women) is often much more subtle than overt wife-beating. In my experience with the Christian misogynist, this subtlety takes on an even more effective disguise. With God on his side, the misogynist has "the ultimate weapon" to keep his woman in "her place"—and he often uses that weapon.

2

THE MISOGYNIST

What does a misogynist look like? What does he do? How can you spot one? In many respects the misogynist is similar to the classic narcissistic personality disorder description found in the *Diagnostic and Statistical Manual of Mental Disorders* used by the American Psychiatric Association.[1] While true narcissists are unable to maintain permanent relationships, misogynists have that ability. The unique feature of misogynists is that their abusive, nonempathetic grandiosity is directed toward the women in their lives. Misogynists may occasionally exhibit these characteristics toward other people, but the brunt of their disorder is aimed at their wives or girlfriends.

Consider some of the characteristics of narcissism outlined in the *Manual of Mental Disorders*. The following are descriptions along with examples I have encountered in my work:

1. Reacts to criticism with feelings of rage, humiliation, or shame, sometimes unexpressed.

Example: An elder in a church is confronted or critiqued by fellow elders at a monthly meeting. Such criticism often concerns minor points of disagreement, but the pastor learns that whenever this individual is critiqued he returns home and beats his wife (who happens to be an organist at the church).

2. Is interpersonally exploitative: takes advantage of others to achieve his own ends.

Example: A Christian businessman, who flaunts his Christianity to associates, is embarrassed that his wife has left him because of his physical and emotional abuse. He tries to reconcile by saying that he's sorry and that he wants her to come home. She learns that his real motivation for reconciliation is to have her at his side when he attends an upcoming out-of-town business conference.

3. Has a grandiose sense of importance, a need to be noticed as special, unique; he even wants his problems to be seen as uncommon, often feeling that only "other special people" like himself can understand his problems.

Example: After falling into into an adulterous relationship, a husband goes with his wife to their priest to confess the indiscretion. He spends a half-hour telling the pastor how he decided to come, how he knew he had failed, and how good he feels that he could come and admit his failure. After the monologue, his wife speaks. She explains that they are there only because their therapist asked them to meet with the priest. It was not the husband's idea. On the way home after the meeting the husband

44

becomes furious with her for telling the priest the whole story.

4. Is preoccupied with fantasies of unlimited success, fame, brilliance, power, beauty, or ideal love. Needs constant attention and admiration.

Example: A Christian activist becomes insanely jealous when his wife receives more media attention than he does. He forbids her to be present when the newspeople come to interview him and orders her to direct all further inquiries from the press to him. He smashes her electric typewriter on the driveway in order "to teach her a lesson for grandstanding."

5. Has a sense of entitlement and unreasonable expectations of especially favorable treatment.

Example: A church elder comes home and finds that dinner is not ready. He flies into a rage even though it is obvious that his wife has been tending four small children all day, all of whom are sick with the chicken pox. He tells her that their illness is "no excuse" and that he expects his dinner on time from now on, no matter what!

Lack of empathy: inability to understand and recognize how others feel.

Example: A Christian physician comes to counseling, complaining that his wife has left him. Nine months later he still "can't understand" why she left him despite the concerted efforts of the therapist, their pastor, and two friends to help him understand that his wife's emotional pain stems from the physical and emotional abuse in their relationship. He says he'd tell her that he was sorry she was hurt, but his "honest" feeling is that it's "just a lot of baloney."

45

These brief examples point out the subtlety and variety in misogynistic behavior. In essence the misogynist is extremely self-centered; yet he is also terrified. He is often the product of a dysfunctional family system. He has never felt secure. While he hates the woman in his life, he is also terrified that she will leave him. His unconscious reasoning goes like this: "If I treat her badly enough, rob her of all self-esteem and confidence, make her physically ill and emotionally dependent on me, then she'll have to stay. She'll never be able to leave me."

UNCONSCIOUS RAGE

Misogynistic men also possess a deep inner rage against women. For most of them, it is an unconscious factor. Despite emotional abuse or neglect by their mothers, they often deny feelings of hurt or anger. In therapy they protest that they had "wonderful" parents or at least parents who "meant well." One man, whose father was a lay religious leader but who beat him cruelly and often, told me with a smile, "I probably deserved every beating I ever got."

CONTROL-ORIENTED

The misogynist is extremely control-oriented; he needs to control and dominate his wife. This is what distinguishes him from a true narcissist who values attention over control. The misogynist has a deep need to rule her every thought, action, feeling, or behavior. One client recently shared with me that her ex-husband, who is a misogynist, has received some counseling and gained new insights about his behavior in their relationship. He admitted that he had treated her badly, as an attempt to keep her from abandoning him. He said, "I was sure that if I let you walk out the door, you would not come back." Out of his fear, he had attempted to control her in every area of her life:

1. He did all the grocery shopping because he would not let her go to the store.
2. He picked out her clothes and gave her his mother's old clothing and shoes to wear.
3. He did not allow her to cut her hair because he liked long hair. If she tried to style her hair according to her preferences, he would fly into a rage.
4. He did not allow her to wear make-up because if she did "she was out to flirt with the other men."
5. He irrationally believed that men who might glance at her when they traveled together did so because they "wanted" her. He beat up complete strangers because they happened to glance at her as they drove by.
6. He never took her anywhere. She ended up being house-bound a year or more at a time. If she had remained in the relationship, she would probably have been committed to a psychiatric hospital.

The misogynist exerts control in the bedroom, too, by regulating their sexual relationship overtly or covertly. Types of sexual control include: limiting or excluding foreplay, subtle or direct sexual criticism, and criticism of her body or the bodies of other women. He may make sex mechanical (when and where he wants it), refuse to be concerned about her sexual satisfaction, become less and less physically affectionate after the wedding, express repulsion or disgust at the idea of romantically touching, or use blame or punishment when her sexual needs differ from his own.[2] One woman reported that she gained ten to fifteen pounds after the wedding mostly because of the stress she felt when her husband picked on her. One day as they walked alone on a beach, he turned, grabbed her abdomen in his fists, and shook the fat, screaming, "There—see that? You're disgusting!" Then he stomped away down the beach. This was the same man fellow church members thought of as the ideal, loving Christian husband!

TWO TYPES OF FINANCIAL CONTROLLERS

The misogynist also extends control over the financial and social aspects of the relationship. In the financial area, Forward points out that there are two types of controllers.[3] The first is the "good provider." He has a stable job, is career-oriented, and is often very successful. However, his attitude is one of dominance and control. He thinks, "I earn it, so I decide how we spend it." In order to keep his wife off balance, he deals with their finances in an unpredictable manner. One day he praises her for going out and improving her wardrobe; the next day he screams at her, throws any purchases on the floor, and insists that she return the items. Meanwhile, he spends as much money as he wants on himself. One woman reported that she had a charge card and her name appeared on the checking account, but if she used either, her husband beat her up. If anyone ever questioned him about his control of the finances, he could reply quite innocently, "She has a credit card, and her name is on the checking account. What more can I do?" This type of misogynist believes that women are innately greedy. He thinks that he must control all of the finances to protect himself from her greed.

Forward's second type of financial controller is the "tragic hero." This man represents himself as hard-working, dedicated, and noble, but he is also the victim of what "others have done" to him. He has financial problems all of his adult life because he handles money like an irresponsible adolescent. Even when his wife assumes the role of primary breadwinner, he blames her for his financial instability. She becomes the enemy. He begins to lie without remorse, behaves in an infantile manner, and refuses to take responsibility for their financial difficulties.

One woman has set up her husband in business at least twice during the twenty-five years of their marriage. The most recent investment initially cost her several hundred thousand dollars. Although the business has broken even throughout the last ten years, it has yet to make a large enough profit to support their family. Thus she has assumed all of the family financial responsibilities. She put their children through college and handles daily living expenses, Christmas celebrations, vacations, and emergency expenses. Yet during arguments, the husband says resentfully, "You're disgusting! You have never contributed anything to this marriage. I work hard all day long and you can't contribute anything!"

SOCIAL CONTROL

In the couple's social life, the misogynist uses a variety of tactics to control his wife's behavior. He must control all social contacts in order to feel safe himself. He allows her to be in touch with only those individuals or groups that support his view of reality. To coerce his wife into dropping relationships which make him personally uncomfortable, he may use rage, temper tantrums, or insults. He may make the social situation so unpleasant that she decides it is not worth the hassle. His tactics include pouting, sulking, refusing to socialize with others, flirting openly with other women in front of his wife, insulting her friends or family members when they are together, refusing to attend functions, or completely dominating conversations or interactions so others do not extend future invitations.[4]

Privately the misogynist undermines his wife's social life by unleashing a small armamentarium of devices: limiting her use of the telephone for local as well as long-distance calls, demeaning her family and friends with the not-so-subtle implication that there must be something wrong with her because she is associated with them, forcing her to quit school or a job or to change churches. Any of these devices may be used directly or indirectly. He might say things such as, "Of course, I want you to finish school. It's just that I'm so miserable when you aren't with me. I need you here by my side. This is where you should be." There is never any question that the woman should yield to the husband's thinking and desires. Anything else would be "rebelliousness" and evidence of an unbiblical lack of submission. The scriptural notion of mutual submission is not present here; thus the woman may feel simultaneously flattered and guilty. She feels complimented that he wants to be with her and guilty that she wants to take classes on two evenings a week.

FAMILY BACKGROUNDS

As mentioned earlier, misogynists have a deep unconscious rage against women. They come from dysfunctional families where they either felt smothered and controlled by the mother or experienced her as weak, passive, and despicable. The father either modeled misogynistic behavior (and the mother took the passive role) or was weak and passive and was dominated by the mother. The son learned to despise women either for their weakness or for their dominance. Often the son is unaware of the emotional abuse or neglect that he experienced. Reaction formation is a common defense mechanism misogynists use toward their families. They consciously express love and admiration for their parents instead of anger, hurt, or pain. If the neglect or abuse is pointed out, they respond with remarks such as, "Oh, that never bothered me," or "Well, they did the best they could; I really love them," or "I probably deserved it—I was a real jerk as a kid." These men learned long ago to suppress their pain and hurt. When they see it in their wives' reactions to them, they often resent it and express rage. It is as if they are threatened by the hurt in their wives because it touches their own deep, internal, unexpressed pain.

A misogynist is often bright and college-educated, so his wife may try to reason with him about his irrational and cruel behavior. The woman fails in her communication attempts mainly because the misogynist does not care. He is so self-absorbed that although he may profess to care about her feelings, in reality he cannot even understand them. His wife's feelings and thoughts have no validity for him. Lack of empathy in general, but particularly toward his wife, is a major hallmark of his attitude. He can be superficially warm and charming to suit his purposes, but this facade is merely a manipulative tactic. He wants his wife to focus on him, not on her own pain. He regards any sign of weakness, hurt, pain, or emotional distress as disgusting, and he doesn't hesitate to let his wife know what he thinks.

THEIR DREAM GIRL

A misogynist unconsciously wants a perfect wife. The woman he idealizes is always a tower of strength: she never has headaches, never gets sick, never has emotional problems, obeys him instantly and without reservation, never questions his decisions or behavior, and is never angry. She is Florence

Nightingale, the Virgin Mary, Wonder Woman, and Betty Crocker—all wrapped into one beautiful package. This ideal woman is able to read his mind and anticipate his needs without a thought for her own needs. If she fails to meet his needs, he responds in a hurt manner, "If you really cared about me, you'd know what I wanted." By holding such a high unconscious standard, it is no wonder that the misogynist is disappointed when his wife fails to make the grade. Yet rather than adjusting his mental and emotional expectations to reality, he clings to these ideals. Perfection is a lot to expect from an ordinary mortal, but the misogynist insists on it and uses his tactics to try to make his spouse shape up. When his wife cannot conform to his expectations; he sees himself as loving, caring, and patient, especially because he has to "put up with such a useless woman."

DR. JEKYLL AND MR. HYDE

Before marriage, during the pursuit and courtship phase of the relationship, Mr. Misogynist looks like Prince Charming. He often sweeps the woman off her feet and pursues her with gifts, flowers, and enthusiasm. She is overwhelmed at all the attention and pushes any doubts under the rug. Many of these marriages begin with a whirlwind romance; it is not until after the wedding that the man's darker side emerges.[5]

One woman reported that the first sign that something was amiss came on their honeymoon. Her new husband screamed at her in rage for getting the shower rug wet when she stepped out of the shower. Another woman told me that her husband flew into a rage whenever the dresser drawer was left slightly ajar. Such overreactions to small matters are typical of the misogynist's need for control. These outbursts are confusing for the wife because they occur in a seemingly haphazard way. What sets him off one day, he hardly notices the next day. One minute he is sweet and charming; the next minute he is enraged.

This type of on-again, off-again behavior traumatizes the misogynist's wife and children. No one ever knows when he will fly into a rage. The wife and children walk around on eggshells. Any confrontation by the woman regarding his inconsistency and temper is met with blame and accusation. The woman begins to believe that she deserves this treatment because her husband seems sure that the only reason he does these things is because of her. This pattern of interaction keeps her off balance—exactly what the misogynist wants.

TOOLS OF THE MISOGYNISTIC TRADE

The tools of the misogynist's warfare are both covert and overt. Sometimes his behavior even looks all right until it is examined as a whole; then the pattern of abuse and control becomes clear. The goal of his emotional and psychological battering is to wear his wife down, to keep her under his control at all costs.

Some of the tools of abuse and control are yelling, bullying, threatening, temper tantrums, name calling, constant criticism, verbal attacks, ridiculing the woman's pain, subtle attempts to confuse her and make her doubt her sanity, forgetting things that happened between them, accusations, blaming, and rewriting history. The misogynist uses all these tactics with the overt aim to "teach you a lesson" or "make you a better person." In Christian homes the justification for abuse becomes even more powerful. Often God or the Bible is used to justify the verbal attack as "correction." "If you were a really good Christian wife you'd . . . ," or "I only do this because God gave me the authority to lead you and be your spiritual head." These become stereotyped defenses. If the wife shows anger, fear, or weakness, she is "rebellious," "untrusting," or "immature in the Lord." If she questions her husband's decisions or opinions, she must be disciplined for her own good. If she turns to the pastor for help, he often reinforces her husband's abuse, albeit sometimes unwittingly. Most pastors do not have specific training to spot emotional abuse; unfortunately, some may be misogynists themselves. Like the alcoholic physician who fails to diagnose the alcoholics in her practice, a misogynist pastor is apt to overlook such abuse. He may even support such men in his congregation.

3

WOMEN WHO MARRY MISOGYNISTS

What kind of woman falls in love and marries a man who hates women? What keeps her in an unhappy relationship? What does she do to reinforce his cruel behavior?

In *Women Who Love Too Much* Robin Norwood discusses the quintessential codependent woman.[1] Frequently she is from a dysfunctional family and has a need to love, to give, to nurture. Early in life she learned to take the role of the responsible child or the placater. She discovered that positive strokes from others were connected with caretaking behaviors, so she learned to repress her needs, feelings, and desires in order to become the model child. Adults would comment that she was "four going on forty." Helpful, kind, caring, always ready to nurture, this woman learned to be obsessed with what others need; meanwhile, she neglected and denied her own needs.

Codependency is a learned pattern of attitudes, feelings,

and behaviors that makes life painful. It leads to a lifestyle in which one's own needs are neglected because one is so deeply absorbed in taking care of others. After a while, the codependent person finds that she has little or no identity apart from those for whom she is caretaking. Codependent behavior that is learned early in life is seen as normal, desirable behavior. When the woman was raised in a Christian environment, such caretaking is often reinforced by well-meaning Sunday school teachers and pastors. It is confused with humility and servanthood.

Melody Beattie comments in her book, *Codependent No More:*

> Others may have interpreted religious beliefs as a mandate to caretake. Be cheerful givers, we are told. Go the extra mile. Love our neighbors, and we try. We try so hard. We try too hard. And then we wonder what's wrong with us because our Christian beliefs aren't working. Our lives aren't working either. Christian beliefs work just fine. Your life can work just fine. It's rescuing that doesn't work. "It's like trying to catch butterflies with a broomstick," observed a friend. Rescuing leaves us bewildered and befuddled every time. It's a self-destructive reaction, another way co-dependents attach themselves to people and become detached from themselves. It's another way we attempt to control, but instead become controlled by people. Caretaking is an unhealthy parent-child relationship—sometimes between two consenting adults, sometimes between an adult and a child.[2]

Codependent Christians usually carry an extra burden of guilt; they take life and Christianity too seriously. Expecting themselves *always* to be helpful, loving, and kind becomes a prison. Caretaking becomes linked closely to martyrdom: taking up one's cross and following Jesus. Self-sacrifice goes out of balance. Rather than living one's life with a sense of peace, joy, and serenity according to a grace theology, the codependent believer is ruled by an iron law of works.

CHARACTERISTICS OF CODEPENDENT WOMEN

Codependency characteristics can affect men as well as women. The concern here is to see how codependency affects women who are married to misogynistic men. A fuller discussion of codependency can be found in my book *Can Christians Love Too Much?* (Zondervan, 1989). The following are some characteristics of such women.

Dysfunctional Family System

Codependent women usually come from a dysfunctional family system. As children these women learned about relationships from watching what did or did not happen between their parents. Usually they picked up a subtle anti-female bias from the type of relationship they observed between their mother and father. Communication in these families often took place in a double bind fashion, causing the child to feel confused and fearful.

The mother might put the child in a double-bind by saying one thing but doing another. For example, the mother would weep bitterly to the daughter about the cruel treatment that she and her daughter receive from her husband, but then refuse to stand up to him directly. She might hold one view of men privately, but her actions demonstrate another. One individual told me that when the women of the family were alone, her mother would comment, "Yah! Men! You have to do everything for them. They can't stand any trouble or disruption!" The message was clear that men were fools, babies, and chickenhearted. In the view of this family, it was

57

the women who were the strong ones. Yet this woman told her daughter over and over, "You'll never make it if you don't have a husband. You have to get married." On one hand, men were the saviors, indispensable elements of a woman's life and wholeness; on the other, men were basically stupid and weak and needed to be coddled.

An aura of uncertainty filled these dysfunctional families. One never knew when Daddy might explode. Yesterday he was nice and calm, even though your toys were on the floor. But today you don't know how he will behave. Sometimes the father was physically or emotionally abusive. In other cases he might have been merely absent in a physical or emotional sense. Women growing up in this atmosphere lived in fear of losing Daddy's love. Sometimes he was mean; sometimes he was nice. The child quickly learned that her behavior was supposed to make the difference (even though in reality it did not). Mother would say that "Daddy only hit you because you are so naughty," or "He's only upset because you . . . ," or "If you would just do what he says, then he'd be nice to us." Yet the meanness would come whether the child was good or bad and then go away without warning.

Needing to repeat the past with desperate hopes of undoing it, women from these types of dysfunctional families are drawn to men who are emotionally and/or physically abusive, or at least negligent.[3] In many cases the mother was a poor model of womanhood, of motherhood, and of being a marriage partner. Obviously, the parental marriage usually had problems, so the situation repeats itself from one generation to the next.

Sandy, like most codependents, found her "nice-guy" first husband "boring." There was no thrill, no zest, no chemistry. They split amicably after five or six years, and she soon found herself attracted to a high rolling, flashy "Christian" businessman. She had recently rededicated her life to Christ and thought that this wealthy, charming, Bible-quoting gentleman was the answer to all her prayers. He swept her off her feet, bought her presents and a car, and rented an apartment for her. He seemed the complete opposite of Sandy's fundamentalist father, who had been a traveling preacher. Sandy's father had made sure that all three of his daughters (and his wife) knew who was boss. Never making enough to support the family, he moved them from "ministry opportunity to ministry opportunity," always promising brighter days ahead. The brighter days never came, and by the time Sandy was eighteen years old she had lived in fifteen different towns. Gruff and hard-driving, Sandy's father insisted that she assist him with his tent meetings. When she was tired or wanted to be with her friends, he labeled her "lazy" and "ungrateful."

Sandy had resolved to leave home as soon as she could. She married the first man who asked her when she was nineteen years old. He turned out to be almost "too nice"; Sandy found herself drowning in boredom. Surely life had more to offer. Sandy found all the excitement she could handle in her second husband. The changes began during the honeymoon. First, he did not want her to work; he wanted her to be available whenever he needed her. Yet when she needed him, he labeled her as "grasping," "insatiable," or "pathetic." He was always "too busy" to listen, just like her dad! Then he began to criticize her every move, just as her father had done all her life. The adoring charmer had disappeared; instead she found a man bent on controlling and correcting her entire life. Just like Dad he used Bible verses to justify his controlling behavior. As their life together progressed, Sandy realized how much her second husband was like her father. A fine Christian veneer covered a layer of emotional and, later, physical abuse.

Easily Deceived

Codependent women are usually easily deceived by the occasional "nice" behaviors that their mates exhibit. Codependents are desperate for love, acceptance, and attention. When someone treats them well—even after terrible abuse a short time before—they lap up the attention like a thirsty puppy. They confuse "niceness" or even merely a lack of abuse with "love," and they convince themselves that, "after all, he does love me." Thus they allow alternating cycles of abuse and niceness to continue.

Example: As a young wife and mother, Elaine wanted nothing more than a "fine Christian home." She worked part-time as the missions coordinator at the church where her husband was the organist; yet no one knew the horror she faced each evening. Not only was her husband a different person with her and their young child at home; he also became physically violent. He screamed at her, threw her against the wall, grabbed her arm until it bruised, kicked her out of bed (literally), and belittled her in front of their child— all without provocation. Like all codependents, Elaine was a people pleaser and tried desperately to "correct" her behavior so as to please her spouse. Yet each time she tried, it seemed as if the rules had changed. The next day he'd be sorry, send her flowers, call her sweetheart, and beg her for forgiveness. Wanting to be a "good Christian," Elaine always forgave him. She told herself, *This time it's different. This time he's really sorry. He even prayed with me! I know he's really changed and that he's seeking God this time.* And so it continued, on and on. Elaine's need for "love"—even at the tremendous cost to her self-esteem—made her keep investing her hopes in his "nice" behavior while she ignored his negative behavior.

Noble Martyr

Codependents may unconsciously see themselves as noble martyrs, whether they play the role of the victim or rescuer in the relationship. This characterization is true of all codependents, but especially Christians. Self-sacrifice is part of the Christian ethic, so codependency fits into the Christian belief system. These women see themselves as helpless "under the mighty hand of God" and forced to be "submissive" to His design for their lives. They believe that there are no alternatives to their situation but to endure, bear their cross, and pray that death or the Second Coming occurs soon. This is not good theology or true servanthood but a form of learned helplessness that is reinforced by their religious belief system. Learned helplessness is observed in victims of chronic abuse or trauma; these people feel that they have no ability to make choices or influence their destiny. They have been subjected to adverse conditions beyond their control for so long that they eventually believe they cannot change their situation in any way. Thus they tolerate abusive circumstances well beyond the limits of a rational individual.

The complementary side of codependents' martyr orientation is their Messiah complex. Codependents receive a powerful emotional reinforcement from their caretaking, overnurturing, and rescuing behaviors. They see themselves as "called by God" to fulfill a certain role, to save or help their errant husbands. They may suffer, but in a lofty and noble cause. "After all, look at all I am putting up with. Look at all I endure. Someday surely I will be rewarded for my patience in adversity." This is exactly what Christianity promises: we may suffer here, but in the "by and by" everything will be set right.

I am not deemphasizing or belittling the importance of biblical doctrines such as the sovereignty of God, servanthood, mutual submission, or the "reward laid up in heaven" for us, but in the mind of a codependent person, these doctrines and others become distorted and are powerful reinforcers of incredibly sick behavior. Christian women who indulge in this masochistic interpretation of biblical doctrine see themselves as noble because of their rescuing and suffering. Unable to see themselves as glorying in this Martyr/Messiah role, they claim that they want help. Yet when help is offered, they refuse it or lapse back into a sick relationship. The comfort of habitual misery and compulsive repetition is common.

Example: When Martie was five years old, her alcoholic mother could no longer care for her. Her father had been killed in Korea, so she was placed in a foster home. Martie married when she was eighteen years old. She was very naïve and sheltered. She did not realize until her husband began to drink years later, that her mother had been an alcoholic. Martie became a Christian at the age of thirty-three. She was sure that with the power of prayer behind her, her husband Wayne would stop drinking. She prayed diligently, and after some time her husband sought treatment. Martie's joy was short-lived. Her husband declared that the treatment was for other people, that he was not like the other people at the treatment center, and that he could handle his alcohol.

In desperation Martie sought counseling. She was sure that if she changed enough, her husband would turn around. However, over the next few years her husband's alcoholic behavior did not change. Martie set up numerous deadlines by which she expected change; otherwise, she said, she would leave him. She vacillated between canceling calls to attorneys, leaving and returning to her husband, threatening and cajoling him to change. Finally her health failed, and she left him for some months. During this time of separation she told herself, *Maybe it wasn't so bad after all. Maybe he is sincere when he says he will change. Maybe now God will change him.* Martie acted helpless when she was with her husband and when she was away from him, yet she seemed to revel in the chaos. Two weeks before her divorce hearing she decided to cancel the divorce and moved back home. Surely God would help her now for being submissive, sticking with Wayne, and not getting a divorce! Today Wayne is still drinking and Martie is still praying.

Self-Blame

Codependents unconsciously blame themselves for everything that happens. They use apologies like a magic wand to ward off anticipated harm. They are the type of people who walk into a room and apologize for breathing too much of the air. Extreme people pleasers, they are sure that their behavior is so powerful that they can, and do, cause other people to fail, behave badly, drink too much, or be cruel to their children. When others blame them for problems, they readily accept that view of the situation. It never occurs to them to question the other person's perception. This automatic self-blaming behavior is particularly true of women in relationships with perceived male authority figures. The biblical injunctions "Be submissive" and "Confess your sins" make such women fearful of questioning the other person, so they avoid asking appropriate questions and apologize instead. The apology is supposed to placate the other person, but it often enrages him further. It is as if the woman's "meekness" and "submissiveness" feeds his cruelty.

Ruth Ellen exemplifies this self-blaming behavior. She was raised in a sheltered home by a passive father and a domineering mother. Her father was an independently wealthy lawyer. Her mom was self-centered and controlling in her relationships with family members. Ruth Ellen played a "Cinderella" role in the family, with her younger sisters getting preferred treatment. Her older brother had died of pneumonia when she was only four years old. A chubby youngster, Ruth Ellen was constantly ridiculed in front of the other family members whenever she ate anything. She learned to hide her chubby form under baggy clothes and prayed to be thinner.

At age 18, Ruth Ellen left home. She enrolled in a strict Christian college, which did not allow dating. But she did become friends with Richard. After completing her nursing degree, Ruth Ellen married Richard. Their relationship was turbulent from the beginning. She desperately wanted a home and a loving family. He was concerned only with status and wealth. Richard was a brilliant scholar and soon earned his Ph.D. and landed a job at a prestigious university. His grandfather had left him a large trust fund, so he was able to combine these funds with his generous salary and live accordingly.

Sexually, the marriage started off on a negative note. Despite Ruth Ellen's pleas for gentleness and romance, Richard virtually raped her on their wedding night. He said that she had kept him waiting "long enough" and that "he wasn't going to wait any longer." So not only did Ruth Ellen feel frightened and hurt, but she felt guilty, too. As the marriage progressed, any sexual problems that arose were always her fault from both her view and her husband's.

Meanwhile, Ruth did everything she could to please her husband. For a while she worked at a local hospital but quit when Richard complained. Soon children were born and though Richard had consented to a family, he ignored them for the most part. When he was in the mood to notice them, he was harsh, critical, and physically abusive. Ruth Ellen was dismayed, but she never thought to question his behavior, since he was the "head of the house." He prided himself on being a born-again Christian and insisted that Ruth Ellen be submissive.

From early in their marriage, Ruth Ellen and Richard attended a fundamentalist church that believed that women should (like children) "be seen and not heard." Ruth Ellen was allowed to attend those church meetings that Richard attended, so that she always would be "under his authority." She never questioned all this controlling behavior because she assumed it was biblical and proper.

Richard, like other misogynists, controlled every facet of their life together—everything from the clothes the children wore to the type of toilet tissue they purchased came under his scrutiny. If Ruth Ellen went over her budget at the grocery store, he became enraged and demanded that she go back immediately and return certain items. However, once when she questioned his purchase of a new sports car, he threatened to hit her.

One day a friend urged Ruth Ellen to read Susan Forward's book *Men Who Hate Women and the Women Who Love Them*. She agreed to read it mainly out of curiosity. She was shocked to realize that she was being emotionally and physically abused in her marriage and that she didn't deserve it. She had told herself for years that if she'd just be a "better wife" and be more submissive to her husband, then God would answer her prayers and make Richard be nice to her. After reading the book, Ruth Ellen decided to talk to a therapist. She had received a small inheritance and planned to pay for her therapy with it. Her husband and the church thought that psychology was from the Devil, so she did not dare tell anyone that she was in therapy. Later she confided in two close friends.

At the beginning of therapy, her therapist realized that Ruth Ellen was severely depressed and on the verge of a nervous breakdown. He collaborated with Ruth Ellen's family physician to prescribe antidepressant medication. Her therapist began to teach Ruth Ellen about human rights and assertiveness, but her misinterpretations about biblical submission in marriage confused her and interfered with this process. Ruth Ellen was convinced that all her problems were due to her spiritual disobedience and her lack of submission. She spent many hours crying and pondering questions such as "Why is this happening to me?" and "What did I do wrong?" Her therapist helped her to look beyond self-blame to other issues, but Ruth Ellen would quickly lapse into her martyr role every time she experienced conflict with her husband.

Ruth Ellen's close friends who knew about her counseling and home situation suggested that she should separate from her husband because of his continuing violent behavior. Her therapist suggested hospitalization because of Ruth Ellen's severe depression and sudden weight loss of 25 pounds. Ruth Ellen told her friends that they needn't worry and refused to be hospitalized. She continued to volunteer to work at the local hospital and even took on additional work. She told her friends that the work was good for her and kept her from feeling sorry for herself.

In therapy, Ruth Ellen went back and forth between denial of codependency and facing the ugly reality of her situation. When in denial, she continued to ask the Lord for what she should do to make her husband love her. When reality became too much for her to handle, she sobbed like a small child. She stopped therapy.

Some weeks later, the local hospital called Ruth Ellen's therapist, as she had asked. Ruth Ellen had overdosed on sleeping pills. By the time the therapist arrived at the hospital,

Ruth Ellen's husband had taken over the situation. He dismissed the therapist from the case. Although Ruth Ellen's friends had tried to seek the pastor's help for their friend, he had refused to become involved in family matters and thought Ruth Ellen needed her husband's discipline. Soon after this incident, Richard was offered a prestigious teaching position in another part of the country, so they decided to move. Ruth Ellen shared with one of her friends before she left that she was certain everything would be okay now because Richard would be happy and that all she needed to do was keep praying and obeying.

Caretaking Behavior

Codependents, from family backgrounds similar to Ruth Ellen's, rescue other people either by subtly excusing their inappropriate behavior, or by directly stepping in and taking charge. Caretaking or rescuing behaviors are at the heart of codependency. We caretake when we do something for others that they should do for themselves; when we insulate them from the natural consequences of their inappropriate behavior; when we own another's problems or feelings; when we say yes although we mean no; when we do more than our fair share; when we help others and neglect our legitimate needs in the process; when we let someone off the hook by blaming ourselves.[4]

Example: A wife is pushed against the wall by her husband. She justifies his actions to herself, thinking, *He only pushed me because he was in a bad mood. If I'd been more sensitive to him, he'd never have done it.* Thus, she encourages future acts of abuse by providing him with excuses for his inappropriate behavior.

Example: One evening a married couple has a verbal fight because the children's toys are on their bedroom floor. The exhausted wife gets up early the next morning, fixes breakfast in bed for her husband, and offers to pack his suitcase for a business trip.

Example: Monica purchases Jason a bouquet of flowers from her yard sale money. Jason doesn't let her spend money from the checking account, but Monica tries to be extra nice to him in the hope that he will adopt a more loving manner. She thinks that her little kindnesses and loving gestures will help him see his unkind behavior more clearly. She tells herself that he doesn't realize how mean his actions are, that he doesn't really intend to act this way.

Example: Marilyn goes to church and pretends that everything is all right, even though she has severe bruises on her back and thighs where her husband kicked her. Her pretty clothes cover the bruises, and she smiles as she and her husband walk into church. No one guesses that every step is painful for her or that her eldest child also has been beaten.

Denial

Codependents tend to deny what is going on around them. Codependent people have a great capacity to defend and delude themselves regarding unpleasant facts about a situation. They seem to believe that if they push things under the rug long enough, the problem will simply disappear. Hence codependents ignore abuse and stay busy so as not to notice it; they become obsessed with caretaking to distract themselves. They develop compulsive behaviors of their own (overeating, gambling, overspending, drinking to excess, volunteerism) but ignore these behaviors in themselves. Codependents believe that things will be better tomorrow, so they pray harder, go to church more often, and repress their hurt and anger. They fail to recognize their own codependency while seeing it in others.

In the course of the relationship with her misogynistic spouse, Mary Dunbar developed a compulsive eating disorder (see chapter 1). She gained twenty to thirty pounds and could not stop eating candy. While she performed the sadomasochistic acts her husband demanded, she would "disassociate" herself from her body. She reported later that it seemed as if "someone else" had done those things. She wanted a "Christian home" so much that for nineteen years she told herself that the abuse was not going on, that they had a "wonderful" family life, that she and her husband "really loved each other."

A child growing up in the kind of environment Ruth Ellen or Mary did or in other dysfunctional families where codependency develops learns some rules:

1. Your feelings do not matter. Pleasing others and soothing their feelings becomes all-important. Peace is to be maintained at any price.
2. No one is there to protect you. "If Mom can't protect herself from Dad's abuse, she obviously isn't going to take care of me."
3. The only way to handle a man's aggression is to give in to it. "Mom stayed married to Dad for thirty years, and he belittled her and treated her mean, so I guess I have to do it too."
4. The most important thing in life, yet the most painful thing, is to have a man. "The world is a scary place, and without a man, women are helpless. Women are dependent and men have all the power, so even if they treat us badly, we have to take it."
5. The way to keep people from abandoning you is to try to be perfect, meet all their needs, ignore your own thoughts and feelings, and, above all, never act as if their mistreatment is that bad.

Obviously these faulty messages program a young woman for heartache and abuse. Unconsciously she is drawn to the kind of relationship she saw acted out in her family of origin. Just as the misogynist lives in reaction to his family of origin, so the woman he marries is trying to recreate her family script. She wants it to come out differently this time; she is convinced that because she can now use love, devotion, and sex, all the respect, warmth, and tenderness that she longed for from her dad will be hers in marriage.

4

ISSUES IN THE CHRISTIAN MARRIAGE

UNIQUE MANIFESTATIONS OF MISOGYNY IN CHRISTIAN RELATIONSHIPS

We have examined the general features of misogyny in a marital relationship. However, there are some unique expressions, within Christian homes, that result from distortions of Christian faith and theology. These distortions play into the already sick relationship, in many cases exacerbating it.

USING THE BIBLE AS A WEAPON

Christians misogynists use the Bible as their main tool to control those around them. The evangelical faith does stress the importance of Scripture; yet these men use it as a weapon

71

to control and manipulate others. By quoting the Bible and referring to its authority, Christian misogynists have a seemingly foolproof weapon in their campaign to control their wives. Christian women also view Scripture as their standard for behavior; so when their husbands use it to point out their failures, they are quick to succumb and condemn themselves. They end up feeling constantly condemned by their spouses, by Scripture, and by God. It never occurs to them to question their husbands' interpretation of Scripture or to decide for themselves whether it is being used appropriately. All too aware of their faults, they see these biblical injunctions as proof that they have failed and that if they would just "do it right," everything would be fine.

As we all know, Scripture can and has been used to justify everything from slavery to the Holocaust. In the hands of a misogynist, we see a more subtle, but nonetheless serious, distortion.

Example: Sandra wants to go to school and finish her bachelor's degree. The two children are in high school, and there is plenty of money for her to do so. Her husband responds, "The Bible says a woman is to be the 'keeper of the home.' There is no way any wife of mine is going to traipse around the campus taking classes! Your place is here at home!"

Example: Mark and Martie plan to attend a new Bible study group. Before they leave home, Mark says, "You know, Martie, that the Scripture says wives are to be silent in church. Well, I think we need to be obedient in this area. So even though this is a Bible study class, I want you to speak only when I give you permission. If you want to speak, look at me, and if I nod, you can go ahead. You are never to pray out loud, because that is a man's job."

Example: Marianne protests when John decides to give

their daughter ten whacks with a hairbrush for every spelling error she makes. (The child usually gets ninety-five to ninety-eight percent of the words right.) John grabs the hairbrush and stomps off toward the child's room, yelling as he goes, "Spare the rod, spoil the child! That is what Scripture says and that is what I say."

Example: Dennis insists that Suzanne participate in a form of sex that she finds repulsive; consequently, she feels manipulated and degraded. She tries to comply but finds herself losing all sexual interest in her husband. Hurt because Dennis is not sensitive to her feelings, she pleads with him to stop demanding that she do it. He responds, "If you were willing to be a good wife like the Bible demands, you'd submit to my desires. No matter how much you don't like it, you'd do it to please me. Instead you are a withholding, rebellious, un-Christian wife. I think you're disgusting!"

USING "GOD'S WILL" TO MANIPULATE

Evangelical Christians have a respect for God and His authority in their lives. Appealing to "God's will," "God's best," "what God would want," or "what Jesus would do" all become powerful motivators. No Christian wants to be "out of God's will" or do something "Jesus wouldn't do"; so compliant, dutiful wives fall into line when misogynists use these phrases whether or not it makes sense, feels right, or seems healthy.

Another way that misogynists commonly manipulate their wives is to grow very solemn and serious, take out their Bible or prayer journal, and proceed to tell them what "God or the Holy Spirit has led me to do." As firm believers in "the priesthood of all believers," Christian wives are drawn easily into such spiritual manipulation. After all, who can argue with the Holy Spirit?

Example: One misogynist kept his wife from establishing any ties with anyone outside the marriage by moving the family every twelve or fourteen months. This pattern did not change even after his conversion. In fact, it became more difficult to fight because now he'd tell her it was "God's will" that they move.

Example: Phillip was separated from his wife for three years, but not divorced, and had an affair with a needy, codependent Christian woman. A Christian himself, he told her that "it was God's will" for them to have sex because "in God's eyes we are already married." She begged him not to do it, but Phillip pressured her and forced himself upon her. Afterward he said he had "no guilt" because "God had created sex and their love was beautiful."

Example: A misogynist in New England, whose wife had left him and filed for divorce, became acquainted with a vulnerable, newly separated woman. A handsome Ph.D., he charmed her, wined and dined her, and asked her to marry him. She agreed happily. As soon as their divorces were final, they were to be married. However, just before the divorce papers were final, his wife changed her mind and begged him to return. He did, much to the chagrin of his fiancée. He wrote her a letter that said, in part, "I will always love you and be glad we had our time together. God has restored my marriage and I hope you can be happy for us."

MISUSE OF BIBLICAL AUTHORITY/ROLES

Besides having a deep respect for Scripture and for God, the evangelical Christian respects authority. All authority figures are seen as receiving their position from God. To question one's parents, the pastor, the policeman, or head of one's country is unthinkable in many Christian homes. The husband is seen as the "head of the home" (though Scripture never uses that phrase; it describes men as "head" of their wives, not the home). He has final authority, and what he says goes! Without debating the merits of this theological doctrine, suffice it to say that it is often abused. Many men use this notion of their sanctioned "authority" to commit atrocities against women and children. For the most part women have been programmed to acquiesce to authority; and when the weight of the church's or God's sanction is added, they do not receive permission to question or offer opposition. Some Christian teachers and preachers advocate these ideas to an extreme. At a national seminar I attended, one well-known Bible teacher said that even if a woman's husband beat her, she would be better off to "obey God," submit to the beatings, and even die than to leave him to seek relief!

UNDERLYING ROOT PROBLEM

Using the Bible as a weapon, especially the concept of "God's will" to manipulate, and misusing the concept of biblical authority are symptoms of deeper problems within the Christian community. These problems are important and need to be addressed. Such issues are particularly relevant in dealing with the misogynistic marriage relationship. It is not my intent to do an in-depth examination of these topics but merely to highlight and illustrate them.

THE CODE OF SILENCE

The first issue is denial. The concept of wife abuse is an anathema to most Christians. The idea of anyone hating someone else, much less men hating women, is difficult for most Christians to understand. Even victims of such abuse find it difficult to conceive. The facade of Christian "niceness" maintained by an abuser at church and in the community confuses his spouse. Besides he is nice even at home—sometimes! He'll lead the family in prayer one minute; the next, he's beating someone black and blue. Or he'll come home after raging and shouting earlier in the day and beg forgiveness, swearing that he has had "a new experience with the Lord" and that now "everything" will be different. Or he may come home and act as if the tirade or beating never happened.

Shame is another reason why denial has such a tight grip on the Christian church. Instead of being a place where people feel safe to expose their painful problems, the church is often a "holier than thou" social club where everyone tries to appear more sanctified than everyone else. If a person can't appear more holy, one certainly doesn't want to appear less holy; so women who are hurting from misogynistic relationships find it almost impossible to summon up the courage to tell anyone.

Mary is a good example of the strength of denial. She was reared in a Christian family in the Midwest, who attended church regularly. On her wedding day she believed that marrying Todd was the best thing that had ever happened to her. Hardly had the rice been shaken from her veil and the couple home from the honeymoon, when Mary began to wonder if she had made a mistake.

At first, Todd would only throw things at the dog or at the wall. Mary attributed his explosiveness to the stress of working on his Ph.D. She tried harder to have everything the way he liked it so that he would have no excuse to get upset. Even though she was working as a secretary to help finance his schooling, Todd rarely offered to help with chores around their apartment and he always expected meals to be ready for him even if he was late.

Mary reasoned that when the degree program was completed and Todd had a job, he would calm down. She stayed out of his way as much as possible and prayed for wisdom to know what would anger him. Even when he threw things at her, she never confronted him or chided him.

After completing his Ph.D, Todd found a job and children came soon after—three of them. Although superficially fond of them, Todd was more concerned with making a good impression at work and at church. He worked hard, and gave lavishly of his spare time at church and was elected deacon and then elder. When he was forty-five years old, he experienced a deep spiritual reawakening at a church revival meeting. He rededicated his life to Christ, and Mary was certain her prayers had been answered. But his abuse did not change, and Mary didn't tell anyone of his cruelty and violence.

Years later and after many transfers around the country and the world, Todd and Mary still looked like a good Christian couple to outsiders. In fact, they even decided to become commissioned as lay missionaries, people who have an occupation but use their opportunities to be lay witnesses in different cultures as a result of their travel.

Since Todd was well paid, Mary could visit back home in the States often. On one visit, Mary decided to visit a therapist who worked with missionaries on furlough. By now Mary and Todd were grandparents and had been married for thirty-five years. For all those years Mary had hoped the marriage would improve, but it never did. Usually she could hide the bruises with make-up or long-sleeved clothing. But last year she had become more concerned because the doctor had diagnosed a hearing loss in her left ear, which he thought might have been due to a car accident or a fall. Not wanting to tell the doctor that Todd had struck her, she said that she had fallen down the cellar stairs. This was the second permanent injury she had received from Todd. Two years earlier he had blinded her in one eye. Now she was beginning to fear for her life.

When the therapist questioned Mary about confronting Todd, she said it always concluded the same way: If she would not do things to anger him, then he wouldn't hit her. She needed to try harder to please him. Unfortunately, Mary only saw the therapist twice. Mary was afraid to stay in the States because of hurting Todd's reputation and angering him. She recognized her life was in danger, but that was the price she had to pay for peace and keeping up appearances.

One problem frequently faced by wives in misogynistic relationships is that when they do tell someone in the church, they are either discounted or not believed. The misogynist looks so good—how could he be doing these things? The wife must be exaggerating; it can't be that bad! The following statements are typical responses that these wives often receive from pastors, pastoral counselors, elders, and even other women:

"You're just tired. Get a good night's sleep and things will look better tomorrow."

"Maybe you need to be a better wife so that he'll be a better husband. You aren't trying hard enough to please him."

"Sounds like you're just too critical and expect too much. Be patient and lower your standards a little."

"Your husband is just being a good Christian by taking charge in the home."

"You wouldn't upset him so much if you'd just be submissive as Scripture says."

"Oh, don't worry. All men lose their tempers once in a while. It goes with the territory."

"You're not being a good wife. If you were, he wouldn't act like this."

"You haven't been praying enough for him. If you were, Satan wouldn't be causing this problem in your relationship."

"All you have to do is trust God. He knows best. It'll all work out. Don't forget Romans 8:28."

"You shouldn't talk that way about your husband. He's a fine Christian man, a leader in our church! Why are you trying to get attention this way?"

"Are you giving him enough sex? Maybe if you were more interested in sex, he'd stop being so upset. All most men need is a warm dinner and a warm wife in bed!"

Silence is not golden when it covers any kind of abuse. However, silence and denial are apt to be the norm until the church becomes a safe place for people to be real.

SEXISM IN THE CHURCH

Like it or not, there is sexism in the church. Many conservative Christians dismiss the idea of sexism as non-Christian, silly, feminist, or irrelevant. They regard themselves as doing things "God's way" and do not see any need to consider whether prejudice has also crept into the pew. Those sensitive to the realities of sexism in our culture realize that it permeates all our institutions, just like any other sinful behavior. Yet even in churches where such sensitivity exists outwardly, sexism is often lurking underground.

The *Longman Dictionary of Psychology and Psychiatry* defines sexism as "discriminatory and prejudicial beliefs and practices directed against one of the two sexes, usually women."[1] It describes a sexist culture as one which "assigns predetermined economic, social, familial, and emotional roles to men and women not on the basis of individual skills but rather on the basis of sexual stereotypes ... and justified by reference to women's reproductive role as child-bearer."[2]

The purpose here is not to rehash the theological debate over the proper role of women in the church. It is to point out that even in so-called "liberated" or more sensitive churches, prejudice against women—and indeed hatred for women—still exists. How is this "Christian" subculture of prejudice manifested?

Example: A pastor, talking to a young couple after church, puts his arm around the young woman, laughs, and says, "Well, Charlie, the way I handle my wife is to toss her down the stairs on her head every once in a while! Straightens her right up!"

Example: Linda comes to the pastor for counseling about her marriage. He smiles at her and tells her in a smug, condescending manner, "Well, honey, the problem with your marriage is you. Your husband means you no harm. He's a fine man. So he loses his temper and flares up once in a while. Just forgive him like a good girl and go home."

Example: A church hires a clergywoman, but tells her that because she is single and has "no family responsibilities," her salary will be $5000 less than other (male) clergy people on the staff with comparable experience.

Sexism permeates our evangelical culture. In some churches it is intrinsic to certain doctrinal positions. The problem is both cultural and religious. It is time for the church to examine its role in maintaining prejudice against women. When we, as Christians, open our eyes to see women as created in the image of God and as equal heirs of God's grace, and then begin to translate that vision into everyday living, misogyny will begin to fade from the church. Christian men are not immune to the family constellations and processes that breed hatred for women. When the church reinforces these prejudices, we are all losers. Under these conditions, when non-Christian men are converted, they carry into their new faith all their old prejudices and hatred against women. Instead of challenging these biases and exposing the root causes (such as fear, low self-esteem, or a need for power), the church often reinforces and in some cases even applauds such reactions.

By remaining silent about sexism, the abused women as well as the church authorities who hear the horror stories become part of the problem. We need to make the Christian community a safe place for both men and women to look at their fears and foibles without condemnation and rejection. It needs to become a therapeutic community for all God's people.

THE SUBMISSION SYNDROME: OUT-OF-BALANCE THEOLOGY

Another root problem in the evangelical church is misuse of the biblical ideal of submission. This concept has been warped and twisted in so many ways that I doubt the biblical authors would recognize it!

Many Christians confuse obedience with submission. Even the traditional wedding ceremony contains the wife's promise to "obey" her husband. Yet Scripture never uses "obey" in relation to wives; it does use the word in reference to slaves and children (Eph. 6:1, 5). Another misapplication of this concept is the assumption that only women are to be submissive. The Bible is clear both in precept and in example that submission is the lifestyle of all Christians. Scripture calls for mutuality in the marriage relationship. We see Jesus, the Lord Himself, submissive to the needs of others, to his parents, to being a servant to His Father's will. Like Him, all Christians are to be submissive. It is beyond the scope of this book to comprehensively discuss the theology of submission, but we need to understand that this concept can be very dangerous in the mind of a misogynist.

The abused Christian woman, who is sensitive and devoted to the Lord, wants to live a life that will honor Him. Add to that the neurotic need to please all authority figures, especially men, and the result is a powerful combination. When these authorities (from whom she desperately seeks approval) call for "submission" and "obedience," the compliant, codependent Christian woman falls quickly into line. Some people wonder how someone like Mary Dunbar could live with abuse for so many years. When I asked her, she replied, "My pastor and my church taught that I should obey my husband in everything; that as the man he was always the final authority and that I was unsubmissive or rebellious if I questioned his actions."

Many women and men have not been taught nor have they seen modeled a message based on the mutual submission called for in Scripture (Eph. 5:21). Our secular culture and our Christian subculture has popularized several models of male/female roles and marriage relationships that are at variance with the biblical teaching on mutual submission. Three dysfunctional models that I have seen include these:

1. The *Authoritarian Model,* also known as "The man is the

boss" model. This is the traditional model that most people grew up with. Many conservative Christians assume that this authoritarian model is the definitive biblical teaching about male/female roles and relationships in marriage and in the church.

2. The *Power behind the Throne Model,* also known as the "Just wait and see, I'll get my own way" model. This version of male/female relationships is a direct offshoot of the Authoritarian Model. Women who are forced to "submit" to their husbands or are not accorded a respectful role in leadership by male leaders may develop a cunning and conniving style of manipulation. These women manage to persuade their husbands and church leaders that the men run things, but actually these women feel they influence the important decisions that are made.

3. The *Competitive Model,* also known as the "I'm just as good as you!" model. In these relationships, men and women vie with one another for status, power, and success. We often see this style in many modern marriages in which couples compete for everything from "Who's the best parent?" to "Who brings home the biggest paycheck?" to "Who is the sexiest and most attractive?"

None of these models represent the proper biblical roles between men and women in marriage and other relationships. There are a number of fine references that discuss the theological and practical aspects of marriage based on mutual submission, which are listed in Appendix C. However, for the woman who has no idea of what a healthy relationship of mutual submission looks like, let me outline a few characteristics:

1. Both partners live in a daily, personal, voluntary

submission to Jesus Christ as Lord and Savior (Eph. 5:21).

2. Love is based on a deep, mutual respect as the guiding principle behind all decisions, actions, and plans (1 Cor. 13).

3. Both partners are aware of their status as "heirs together" in Christ (1 Peter 3:7) and as equal members of the body of Christ (1 Cor. 12), members uniquely gifted by God's Holy Spirit. Both recognize that the purpose of those gifts is to build up, through mutual submission, the body of Christ as well as their own relationship.

4. Natural abilities and talents of each individual, as well as spiritual gifts, are a practical basis for delegating various roles and responsibilities in the home.

5. The emphasis is on a mature relationship between two adults, not on prescribed, arbitrary roles or functions into which each personality is forced to fit. The marriage is seen as a relationship rather than as a career or an organization.

6. Each person maintains their own God-given personal identity and personality. The concept of being "one flesh" does not mean that each individual has lost his individuality or uniqueness.

7. The sexual relationship is not only procreative but it is one of joy, fun, fulfillment, and refreshment for both partners.

8. Intimacy and deep emotional closeness replaces game playing and role playing.

9. Honesty and fidelity are the cornerstones of healthy communication patterns, based on a deep, abiding trust in the other person and in Christ.

10. Decision-making is based on a process where both

partners have a willingness to come to a mutually satisfying outcome. Consensus is the goal in all matters of importance, and neither party manipulates the other to force agreement. Each person has areas of authority and responsibility where they themselves make decisions based on their gifts, talents, and expertise in those areas. When consensus does not come immediately, the matter is committed to prayer and is not acted upon until there's agreement.

People who are drawn to leadership roles in certain churches or who are attracted to authoritarian interpretations of Scripture become another factor in this equation. Personality does affect theological leanings. People who like things to be right or wrong, black or white, with no gray in between are likely to emphasize biblical issues in the same all-or-nothing manner. People who allow psychological or theological openness in themselves are apt to be more permissive and to encourage openness in others.[3] Those drawn to leadership usually have a need to control, to have power over others. Persons in whom this need is strong feel threatened if others think for themselves, have their own ideas, or ask too many questions. They are more apt to be psychologically (and theologically) closed-minded.

Persons who are oriented toward power and control are easily drawn to professions and/or positions that are socially sanctioned and allow them to take charge of others. These people are drawn to careers as law enforcement officers, military officers, or ministers in authoritarian-style churches. These types of roles have authority and are approved socially. Clergy have a special advantage; if someone dares to question them, they can quickly point to their spiritual and social authority and quench all dissent with scriptural logic, fear, and/or guilt.[4] People with this personality type enjoy the "iron sharpening iron" that occurs in adversarial situations. They like it when only one person can "win"; in fact, they often frame interactions in a "win/lose" manner. Such people want to exert influence by using power and control. They know how to manipulate and get what they want and are not above using intimidation to get it. They are good at threatening another person's self-concept or hooking into another's deepest fears to achieve their own goals.[5]

All of these characteristics are found in the typical misogynist. This type of personality pattern expresses itself in all the misogynist's human relationships, at home, at the office, or in the pastorate. It is easy to understand why the pastor and the elders of Mary Dunbar's church all felt comfortable in believing her husband's story that his abuse was due to her "unsubmissiveness." Unfortunately, circumstances conspired to surround Mary with people who needed to control others, particularly women.

DEEPER NEEDS

What we see is a biblical concept out of balance: certain women with a neurotic need to seek approval from male authorities, and certain men who need to control and dominate others, particularly women. The irony is that despite their outward differences, the deeper needs of misogynistic men and codependent women are similar. Noted therapist Paul Tournier comments about this seeming difference in people:

> The truth is that human beings are much more alike than they think. What is different is the external mask, sparkling or disagreeable, their outward reaction, strong or weak. These appearances, however, hide an identical inner personality. The

external mask, the outward reaction, deceive everybody, the strong as well as the weak. All men, in fact, are weak. All are weak because all are afraid. They are all afraid of being trampled underfoot. They are all afraid of their inner weaknesses being discovered. They all have secret faults; they all have a bad conscience on account of certain acts which they would like to keep covered up. They are all afraid of other men and of God, of themselves, of life and of death. . . . What distinguishes men from each other is not their inner nature, but the way in which they react to this common distress . . . among human beings there are two opposing types of reactions to the same inner distress: strong reactions and weak reactions.

The strong reaction is to give ourselves an appearance of assurance and aggressiveness in order to hide our weakness, to cover up our own fear by inspiring fear in others, to parade our virtues in order to cloak our vices. The weak reaction is to become flustered, and thus to reveal the very weakness we want to hide; it is to allow our consciousness of our weakness to prevent us from bringing into play the concealment-reactions which permit the strong to dissimulate their weakness. . . . In reality we all react strongly or weakly, according to circumstances, but in varying degree.[6]

Both the misogynist (what Tournier would call the "strong" type) and the codependent woman (what Tournier would call the "weak" type) have common root fears and needs. A central fear for both types is the fear of abandonment. Underlying both the domineering stance of the misogynist, who insists that his wife "submit" to him, and the overcompliant nonassertiveness of the codependent woman is a terror that if they do not control/give in, then they will be abandoned.

Thus, the issue is not so much the theology of submission per se, as the psychological openness of those who hold certain views of submission. When we are unaware of our psychological biases, they are more likely to operate destructively. Helping couples and churches to examine the needs and fears underlying particular theological stances would seem to be a first step toward balance.

THE SALVATION SYNDROME

The "salvation syndrome" is another problem that exacerbates the misogynist/codependent relationship.[7] For the most part we have addressed couples who were both Christians at the time of marriage or who both came to a similar commitment later on, but in some cases the marriage begins with one partner a Christian and the other an unbeliever. Typically the scenario goes like this:

Sally, a young, college-educated woman, meets Peter at work. He is a nice, clean-cut fellow and begins the romance. He is much more interesting and exciting than the fellows she has met at church. He is confident, debonair, thoughtful, and fun. Sally is swept off her feet! There's only one problem: Peter is not a born-again Christian. He is moral, in fact in many ways more moral than some of the Christians she has dated. He seems open to her faith, and Sally hopes that perhaps under her influence Peter will come to know Christ. Unconsciously she begins to think of herself as Peter's savior or rescuer. Her love will show him what Christians are really like. They get married. When the honeymoon fades and Peter's darker side begins to show, Sally redoubles her efforts to show Christian love and patience. She attempts to "turn the other cheek" and to forgive "as Christ forgives."

Her pastor and her Sunday school teacher reinforce this attitude, telling her that if she prays harder for Peter, tries not to upset him, and above all does not grow angry in return, God will reward her when Peter "finds Jesus."

Sometimes men like Peter *do* "find Jesus" through their wife's example, but rarely does the misogynistic pattern change. Instead, the newly converted misogynist acquires a larger arsenal: God, the Bible, the pastor's and elders' approval and authority, fear, guilt, and much more.

What is wrong with this salvation syndrome? Primarily it is a delusion. A woman in a misogynistic relationship may believe that she can change or "save" her husband by being sweet, submissive, and passive, but the reality is that this tactic does not work. She must realize the misogynist's emotional investment is maintaining his stance. The misogynist's deepest fear is abandonment. He believes that the best way to keep his woman from leaving him is to cripple her emotionally, to limit her activities, and to keep her guessing psychologically. He does this by using the variety of tactics previously discussed. The goal is to keep her in her place so he will not have to be alone. This action is unconscious; outwardly he appears to be in control, the ultimate master of his fate. This type of person will likely use God, salvation, the church, and even conversion itself as more powerful ways to protect himself from abandonment. He may experience a conversion, but he will not alter his life game plan because of that conversion per se. In my experience, the misogynist must lose or almost lose his wife because of his behavior before he becomes honest enough to face his deepest fear and *truly* experience God's grace.

Another problem with the salvation syndrome is that it reinforces the wife's codependency. On one hand the codependent person sees herself as the victim, the martyr, the one called to suffer, and on the other, as the righteous one, the savior, the "Messiah," the one who is "right" (and righteous).

There is a moralistic, "holier-than-thou" aspect to being a victim. She may seem helpless outwardly, but inwardly she feels an odd exhilaration at being the right one, whom God will vindicate "someday." The "salvation syndrome" reinforces this victim/messiah role. Instead of "letting go and letting God" work, as the recovery programs suggest, the "salvation syndrome" keeps the woman convinced that she *can* change her husband if she prays hard and is "nice" enough. This syndrome can also apply to a woman married to a "backslider" or spiritually lazy Christian misogynist. She may not feel a need to "save" him in the salvation sense, but she is attracted to the idea of "helping him rededicate his life to the Lord."

This salvation syndrome also keeps the woman passive in the sense that she continues to do the same old things to appease or mollify her husband while praying for a miracle. She keeps hoping that God will act, while refusing to take the necessary action to confront her husband in order to change the dynamics of the situation. She fails to understand that perhaps one way God will use her to "help" her husband is by refusing to be abused, and if necessary, by leaving him.

THE DIVORCE DILEMMA

The Christian community must also come to grips with the problem of divorce when dealing with misogyny in the Christian marriage. No one who takes Scripture seriously is apt to take divorce lightly. There are sincere differences in interpretation around this issue, but certain principles are generally agreed upon in most evangelical churches. All of us want to see marriage held in honor. We want to preserve it as a sacred trust, a symbol of Christ's unity with His bride, the church. Even conservative churches allow for divorce in the case of infidelity, usually with the provision that all attempts to heal the relationship have failed. Adultery does not *have to* mean that a marriage is dissolved; neither does the presence of misogyny. The concern is that well-meaning friends and church staff members may unwisely counsel a woman to stay in an abusive situation when leaving is the best option. Leaving may or may not mean a divorce; however, sometimes divorce is necessary to protect the woman and her children from the misogynist's intimidation.

Even the most conservative woman who opposes divorce may divorce with a clear conscience. Sometimes a woman decides to leave and subsequently divorces her misogynist husband for legal reasons. Then she chooses to live celibate before the Lord. The reasoning is this: She still sees herself as married before God, no matter what the legal situation. She chooses not to date or remarry, always allowing for the possibility that God may use even the divorce to bring healing to their relationship.

Certainly it is not God's will for anyone to live in terror or in fear of abuse, whether mental or physical. Every effort should be made to help a couple caught in a misogynistic pattern to find healing. Often this is not possible, mainly because of the misogynist's investment in keeping things as they are. In such cases a woman must decide what she can tolerate without sacrificing her physical and mental health. Unfortunately, many Christians take the phrase "for better, for worse, 'til death do us part" to mean "Stay in your relationship even if it destroys you." One noted Christian author lived for many years with a misogynist. After years of deep struggle and many psychogenic illnesses, she decided to leave her husband. To her great shock, some Christian friends let her know subtly (or not so subtly) that it would have been "better" if she had chosen to *kill herself* rather than to leave!

This sentiment seems extreme, but I believe it reveals the deep sense of shame that Christians feel even in contemplating divorce. Even death by one's own hand seems more respectable! Surely this solution (and attitude) is not one that our Lord would sanction.

None of us wants to liberalize the church's stance on the sanctity of marriage or on the undesirability of divorce. It is always preferable if a couple can work out the issues. (Divorced, they will probably repeat the same pattern anyway.) Yet sometimes this ideal is not possible. We must find ways to uphold a high standard for marriage but allow compassion for human failures.

5

ROOT PROBLEMS: SHAME AND FEAR OF ABANDONMENT

Two issues that lie beneath the dysfunctional relationship between the misogynist and his wife are shame and a fear of abandonment. Both carry deep shame and are terrified of abandonment. These two issues must be addressed for them to experience healing as individuals and as a couple. Often this fear and shame, though an active part of their lives since childhood, remained disguised or ignored.

What Is Shame?

Western culture does not usually distinguish the concept of shame from the concept of guilt. Most Westerners think that the two words can be used interchangeably, though shame might be viewed as a more superficial form of social embarrassment. Guilt is seen as more deeply personal.[1] In other cultures, shame is the predominant feeling. From a

Christian perspective, Scripture puts more of an emphasis on shame than guilt.

In the West, guilt is viewed as an individualistic trait. A person is guilty after violating or crossing some sort of boundary. Guilt is a legal and moral concept that is related to law-breaking and transgression. A person who *is* guilty may or may not *feel* guilty. For example, you might decide to walk against the red light at 2:00 A.M. because no one else is on the road. Technically, you are guilty of breaking the law, but you did not feel any guilt. Or, a person might mistreat his wife or child but feel no guilt because he believes that they deserve it.

Shame is a more social and less individualistic concept involving feeling afraid of criticism from oneself and/or one's peers. To feel ashamed we must perceive ourselves to be observed, even if the observer is only ourselves.[2] Thus, a person can feel shame over events that no one else knows anything about. We often speak of shame with phrases such as: "I was stripped of all my defenses" or "I felt naked or exposed. . . ."[3]

In Genesis 3, we learn about how Adam and Eve sewed together fig leaves to cover their shame. They had broken a law that God had established for them. They were guilty in a legal, moral sense. In addition, they felt shame: they were exposed as being finite, fallible, and as less than they could, should, or wanted to be. They felt shame even before God confronted them. Thus, they experienced disgrace in their own eyes and then before God.

The type of shame mentioned above is what I call "being in a shame state." Adam and Eve, because of their disobedience, not only were guilty before God, but entered into a state of shame. As their descendants all of us are in this shame state prior to salvation. This shame state leads to a pattern of "lifestyle shame responses." The left column of Figure 2

FIGURE 2

SHAME STATE
VS.
SHAME EXPERIENCES

A Shame State Leads To:	Particular Shame Experiences Lead To:
Lifestyle Shame Responses	**Particular Shame Responses**
Hiding our weaknesses	Blushing when your fly is down
Blaming others	Stammering when the teacher calls on you and your mind goes blank
Projecting our shame on others	
Defensiveness	Lying to your father about your grade on a test
Becoming critical of self and others	
Perfectionism	Refusing to date after a rape experience because you feel like "damaged goods"
Works-orientation	
Fear of closeness	Changing your name to "Rose" from "Rojas" because of shame over your cultural heritage
Keeping others away or at arm's length	
Power/control tactics	Dressing frumpily and plainly because of embarrassment over being a woman
Compliant/overly obedient	
People-pleasing	
Being "nice" all the time	
Judgmental behavior	

shows the lifestyle shame responses caused by our shame state.

Being in a shame state differs from the particular shame experiences that we encounter in everyday life. Shame experiences may or may not involve moral or ethical issues. For example, if you are unexpectedly asked to speak in front of a group or someone informs you that your zipper is unzipped, you are likely to experience shame or embarrassment. Such incidents produce shame but do not involve guilt. These types of experiences are usually related to social or emotional situations, rather than personal guilt. The right column of Figure 2 shows the reactions that we have to these "particular shame experiences" in contrast to "lifestyle shame responses" found in the left column.[4]

In a dysfunctional marriage relationship, even when the partners are Christians, we frequently see both types of shame responses: lifestyle shame responses and particular shame responses. Many Christians do not understand that Christ has removed both shame and guilt through His atoning work. They live as if their shame state has not been changed to a mercy state. Thus they continue to live with shame at the center of their lives. In addition, they haven't learned to apply God's grace to themselves and others in the shame experiences we all encounter everyday.

What Is Abandonment?

Most people only think of abandonment in extreme terms. We hear about newborn infants that are left in restrooms or of a parent who runs off and never returns to the family. Thus when we speak about "fear of abandonment," the average individual thinks, "Oh, that doesn't apply to me. My parents were always there in the home. I was never abandoned."

It's more helpful to regard abandonment as a situation in

which the child's needs go unmet. Needs may go unmet because of actual desertion, but there are many other less drastic circumstances that contribute to a sense of abandonment. For example, a father may have had to work two jobs to support the family so he was not at home to nurture and bond with the children. Or a mother, because of her own depression, may have been unable to connect emotionally with her children. Sometimes children experience abandonment (neglect of basic needs) because the parent(s) died or were alcoholics or sick and were emotionally unavailable. Some people experience neglect of their basic emotional needs rather than physical deprivation such as hunger or physical abuse. Perhaps Mom and Dad were physically around, maybe they provided a lovely home, wonderful material possessions, and a good education, but they were emotionally unavailable. They didn't provide enough guidance, affection, affirmation, encouragement. Somehow children "know" that they were loved, but they report that they "never felt loved."

Neglecting children's basic needs has the same effect as if they were physically abandoned. No one is there *for* the children at an emotional level. The children are in some way "on their own." Often children actually take on adult responsibilities and even care for the parent. This type of neglect is not always intentional or malevolent. Sometimes neglect occurs because the family is large and there are too many children to care for, or because of illness or death in the family.

The point is that such children end up feeling all alone with no one there to protect them. These children mistakenly blame themselves for this abandonment. They unconsciously reason that "Mom and Dad are all-powerful. They are wiser, bigger, and better than me, and they take care of me. So if they don't help me, protect me, or take care of me, then it must be my fault. I must be unworthy of such love and attention. I must be no good, unlovable, bad; otherwise, they would be taking care of me. It's my fault."

This unconscious inner dialogue is the only way a child can make sense of such experiences. From a child's point of view, parents are like gods. Parents are perfect and they must be right about everything. So when a child experiences the parent as absent, neglectful, cruel, uncaring, or distant, the child concludes that it is not because the parent may be something inappropriate, but it is because there is something wrong and unworthy about him. The child begins to believe that he is undeserving of care, unworthy of love, and that he should not count on someone being there for him. Thus the child is caught in a terrible and destructive double bind. On one hand, he has real human needs that are unmet (Figure 3); on the other hand, he believes that he does not deserve to have those needs met. People usually deal with this kind of conflict by burying their needs and pretending that their needs aren't real or legitimate. If they feel rejected and abandoned, they consciously mitigate the pain by ignoring their needs and the hurts. Their unconscious dialogue goes like this: *If I ignore these fears and needs, maybe they'll go away.* Yet deep inside, they harbor the fear that someday someone else important in their life will abandon them again.

This is what happens to people who later develop a misogynistic relationship with a spouse in marriage. They have an inner sense of abandonment from the past and a fear that they will once again be abandoned.

FIGURE 3

BASIC HUMAN NEEDS

PHYSICAL:	stimulation/touch, being held, caressed; medical care; food; warmth; shelter; clothing; water; sexual contact.
MENTAL:	stimulation/excitement/challenge; pleasure; pain; play; security; peace of mind; boundaries.
SOCIAL:	structure; limits; predictability; consistency, attention; being regarded as special; guidance; modeling, identification with significant others; time with significant others, feedback.
EMOTIONAL:	affirmation of needs and feelings; encouragement; praise; warmth; affection; sense of self as separate from yet cared for by others; sense of uniqueness and worth, of being wanted or valued for oneself.
SPIRITUAL:	grace, mercy, forgiveness; redemption, repentance, sanctification; maturity; gifts of Holy Spirit; ultimate glorification.

UNMET NEEDS AND THE MISOGYNISTIC MARRIAGE RELATIONSHIP

The Link Between Shame and Fear of Abandonment

Imagine this scenario: A child is born into a dysfunctional family. The parents while well-meaning are ill-equipped for parenting. This child's basic human needs go unmet in a variety of ways. The child begins to feel ashamed of being who he is.

Since attachment to Mother is insecure, this child experiences a high degree of separation anxiety. Love is presented conditionally, based on "being good." When the child is "bad," love is withdrawn and the dreaded separation/abandonment is experienced. The child eventually learns to numb all feelings so as to be unaware of the unmet needs. A phony self is presented to the world, a self that is usually compulsive in some manner. Depending on circumstances, environment, and personality, the child will use one of two styles to cope with his shame: the "Rock" style or the "Sponge" style. The Rock is exhibited by the person who says, "I'm fine. I don't need anybody. I'm no wishy-washy sissy. Sure my folks had problems. It didn't bother me. I can take care of myself." The Rock-style person tends to be persuasive, manipulative, able to get his way. Usually quick thinking and verbally fluent, he tends to dominate or overpower others in any way he can. He is totally unaware of the hurting child buried beneath the Rock. In contrast, the Sponge-style person is a sensitive, emotional, people-oriented individual, who is extremely sensitive to criticism and rejection. He views himself as needy, fearful, timid, overwhelmed, and vulnerable. He experiences his own pain *and* everyone else's (hence the Sponge designation). These types are people pleasers par excellence. Unlike the Rock who does not appear to need *anyone's* approval, Sponges are desperate to please, placate, and perform. Both may be perfectionists, but their responses to failures and mistakes are very different. The Rock just presses on, determined to overcome any and all obstacles to success. The Sponges take the defeat personally and often become caught in a quagmire of self-doubt and self-hate. Sponges are only too aware of their needy inner child and respond by trying to ignore or annihilate it.

It is not difficult to guess which style the misogynist develops and which one his spouse uses. However, underneath the diverse styles is the same fearful, abandoned, neglected, broken child. Both have basic unmet human needs and are terrified of being abandoned and rejected. The woman (with her Sponge-style) and the man (with his Rock-style) operate out of a shame-based personality. Their fear of abandonment and deep shame over who they are (and are not) keep them bound in their own styles of compulsive "acting out." The woman acts out by compulsive people-pleasing, taking abuse like a "good victim" and by chronically neglecting herself. The man acts out by bullying, controlling, acting superior, and manipulating. Both are convinced (unconsciously) that if they do not act the way they do, chaos will result (i.e., they will be abandoned).

Defensive Strategies

To defend themselves from their shame and fear of abandonment, both the man and the woman develop defensive strategies. They use these strategies to pretend they have no shame.[5] Figure 4 lists the strategies they use. These styles are ones we have identified as characteristic of a misogynistic relationship.

Defensive Strategies Of Men and Women In Codependent-Misogynist Relationships

Both Persons	Man	Woman
Perfectionism: Never feeling that anything is good enough. Always comparing oneself to others. Only feeling valued for performance causes one to project a rigid, controlled image. Others hesitate to get close.	Striving for power and control: becomes a way to be sure that no one shames or abandons him.	Caretaking/helping; focuses on others' needs. She can ignore her own pain.
	Rage: keeps others, especially his wife, from getting too close.	People-pleasing: her goal is to get others to like or accept her.
	Blame and criticism: transfers his shame to his partner.	Being nice: a way to manipulate others, avoid shame, and avoid real intimacy.
	Arrogance: helps him forget his shame. He alters his moods by exaggeration.	Envy: discomfort at others' good fortune, feeds self-pity, focuses on them, not on her own situation.
	Judgmentalism and moralizing: A way to win and control others. Especially in the spiritual area. "I" have the correct theology, interpretation, etc.	Taking the blame: keeps her busy feeling guilty so she can continue to shame herself.
	Contempt: utter rejection of other's beliefs and personhood.	
	Patronizing: lets him feel a sense of superiority.	

Boundaries

Another issue related to separation/attachment and fear of abandonment is that of boundaries. In a misogynistic relationship it is as if the boundaries between wife and husband are simultaneously too strong and yet nonexistent. In one way, the misogynist builds walls around himself to keep the woman away, fearing that if she gets too close she'll notice his shame. His bullying has a two-sided purpose; it serves to control her and keep her from abandoning him, but also keeps her at arm's length emotionally. In one way, he comes across as the self-made man, independent, self-assured, confident, needing no one. Yet he is so insecure, so unsure of himself, so unable to separate from her that he sees her, totally and only, as an extension of himself. He is incapable of seeing her as a separate human being. To maintain his security, her boundaries must merge with his and she must become *him*. Any of her activities or behaviors that even hint at differentiation or separation from him and his view of her become intolerable.

The woman also experiences this boundary problem. She is needy, vulnerable, weak, and a victim, who is unable to separate herself from the "love" and attention of a man. Her worth and sense of self is so shaky that she only sees herself as valuable when tied to him in some way. This woman lets his personality overwhelm her and gives way to the force of his persona. Having little ego strength of her own, she leans on his bravado, mistaking it for strength. She has never learned to hold her own with a significant other, particularly a male. Often unaware that boundary-keeping is possible, she blindly plays victim and loses more and more of herself day by day.

In summary, the misogynist and the woman he marries both have boundary problems. Their inability to form secure attachments during childhood and the anxiety/fear they have regarding separation/abandonment make them prime candidates for a dysfunctional marriage relationship. The shame-based behavior patterns they developed cripple them and damage their ability to relate intimately. They develop compulsive coping styles, which are self-perpetuating and self-destructive. Not knowing how to act differently, they continue these behaviors despite the pain.

One task of the healing/therapy process is to address these root problems—teaching the couple new ways to handle shame and fear of abandonment. Identifying the issues is not enough. Each person must develop a new way to live.

6

A WORD TO THE MAN / A WORD TO THE WOMAN

A WORD TO THE MAN

If you are a man whose wife insisted you read this book or you decided to read it on your own, congratulations! Many men would not even allow themselves the freedom to entertain the thought of reading a book on misogyny!

Perhaps some of you have seen yourself in this book. If so, I imagine you feel some embarrassment and shock. Sometimes when someone other than our spouse uncovers our negative behaviors, we are able to view them more objectively. Yet, that process of self-recognition is very painful and you may be experiencing some shame.

Shame is a sense of lowered self-esteem because a person has recognized *I am not what I want, should, or could be.* You may only be scratching the surface of your negative behavior patterns, and even that superficial glance is humiliating. You may feel embarrassed and ashamed of how you behave.

At this point, I urge you to remember John's admonition in his first letter: "My dear children, I write this to you so that you will not sin. *But* if anybody does sin, we have one who speaks to the Father in our defense—Jesus Christ, the Righteous One" (1 John 2:1, italics mine).

When Christ died, He died to take away our shame as well as our guilt. As children many of us learned to shame ourselves when we failed. It was not just that we "made a mistake"—we *were* a mistake. We were shamed by parents who confused our negative behavior with being "bad" (i.e., worthless, stupid, of no value). Whether they meant to or not, many parents modeled self-shaming behaviors to us.

You need to deal with this shame as part of your healing journey. In the past, you unconsciously used bullying and manipulation to handle it. Somehow you learned that keeping people dependent on you or in awe of you made you feel more powerful and worthwhile. And for a few minutes or hours, the shame seemed to disappear. However, like any fix, that powerful high did not last, and shame raised its ugly head again. And so the bullying and controlling continued. The core of your behavior is your fear of abandonment and the shame you feel for being who you are (or who you are not).

I urge you to get professional help from a therapist who understands misogyny. You will be tempted to fall back into old ways of dealing with your pain. Your own deep fears and hurts have caused you to interact with your wife as you have. Uncovering these unconscious feelings will not be easy. The old habits of handling your feelings will seem much more comfortable than the new ways you need to learn. You will need support and encouragement from a therapist and hopefully other recovering men. You may or may not be able to restore your marriage, depending on the degree of damage that has been done. Yet I urge you to work on *yourself*. Only as you work on yourself under the instruction of the Holy Spirit can healing for you and your marriage take place. Do not try to change just to "get my wife back." Commit yourself to change for your own sake and for the sake of the Lord Jesus.

JIM AND BETH ANN'S STORY

Jim and Beth Ann had been married for thirty-nine years. They had reached a point of deep despair in their marriage due to the bitterness, rejection, and mutual sense of failure that they felt about their relationship. Beth Ann was a passive, codependent woman, who had desperately tried to conceal the turmoil of their troubled relationship from friends, neighbors, and even their children. As a Christian woman, Beth Ann had prayed and prayed about their problems. Yet, even in her prayers, she had fooled herself by discounting the seriousness of their relationship difficulties. Her codependent efforts to conceal the problems of her marriage from her children backfired. Her conscious desire to "protect" the children was actually destructive. Only later was she able to see that she had modeled passive behavior as an acceptable relationship style and had portrayed abuse as tolerable.

Finally, after years of emotional abuse, Beth Ann left Jim. She was filled with hurt and deep sorrow. She grieved for the lost years, for her children, and for Jim, who had no idea of how destructive his behavior had been. She was angry with God, because despite her earnest prayers and her counseling with church pastors, their marriage had not improved. Beth Ann did not have the courage or skill to confront Jim about his abusive behavior until it was too late. Beth Ann could see that her passivity in the relationship had contributed to their problems. But she was so numb from the pain, that she only had enough energy to leave home.

Once Beth Ann had moved out, she felt a relief from the enormous tension of the relationship. But she still cared for Jim, even if his behaviors made him a very unlikable person to live with. Separation had never been an option for her before, but now that she was away from Jim and not obsessed with him, she began to experience a new dependence and trust in the Lord. Yet she remained bewildered; her future seemed uncertain. She knew that she couldn't change Jim, yet she was not willing to return to him unless he did change.

JIM TELLS HIS SIDE OF THE STORY THIS WAY:

Two years ago, I lost the most precious thing in my life— my Beth Ann. It didn't happen all of a sudden; this loss occurred over the course of thirty-nine years of marriage. Actually it began when I was a young child. But it was not until recently that I understood the origin of my problem. My mother, though kind and caring, could not show love. I received more than my share of harsh punishment from my father. As a result of my mother's aloofness and the harshness from my father, I was determined that nothing or no one would ever hurt me again. I became a tough character with a "spit-in-your-eye" attitude.

After I married Beth Ann and we had kids, I became strict with the children, who in turn became resentful and rebellious. Our pastor once told me that I was "an angry man"— and I was! Even though I was a born-again Christian, I was filled with anger. Subconsciously angry with my parents for the rejection and hurts of my early life, I read rejection into Beth Ann's actions. Eventually, that became a self-fulfilling prophecy. She was passive-aggressive and unable to communicate constructively or assertively. We went from therapist to therapist, making temporary strides but inevitably falling back further than before and becoming increasingly disillusioned with our relationship. Finally there was nothing left, nothing to look forward to. My impending retirement, instead of being a joyous and happy occasion, began to be a threat. It was at this point that Beth Ann left me.

Suddenly my whole world collapsed. While I could not stand living with her, the thought of losing her was like a death sentence. She left convinced that I would be so hurt and angry that I would never reconcile. I, in turn, felt that my worst fears had been proven: Beth Ann did not love me and she would never return. I felt abandoned. I had never learned to cry. Oh, I cried for my children or Beth Ann if they were ill, but I had never cried for myself. After all, men aren't supposed to cry, are they? Suddenly deep wells of tears opened up within me. I didn't have any contact with Beth Ann for six months. That solitude made me face myself. What came forth was a gusher of pain and hurt. It was as if my guts were being wrenched apart. I hurt physically like I had never hurt before. During the next six months I would weep over and over, prostrate on the floor before the Lord, with no warning of when the tears would come. It was the most devastating period of my life.

After Beth Ann had left I began to talk to God out loud. I remember one occasion when I was all alone in that big empty house; there wasn't anyone else to hear or listen. I asked for peace and insight and begged for forgiveness. Eventually I stopped talking and "listened" for God's response. I didn't hear a voice, but God did speak to me. During the next two-and-a-half hours I was faced with all of my faults in the marriage, as well as with some hints on ways to correct them.

There were many more sessions of prayer and listening in the months that followed. God showed me how I needed to change. I found that the only person I would ever be able to change was myself, so I set out to do so. I gave Beth Ann space and freedom. I didn't initiate any phone calls or visits, but I did assure her that I was available if she wanted to contact me. I realized that throughout our marriage I had selfishly insisted on my own way in so many things, instead of giving freely to her. Whenever I was hurt or angry, I would avoid her for days or weeks. I would withdraw love, attention, and warmth; I would even refuse to converse with her. I had used words as a battering ram to smash her self-image. Gradually I began to make changes. The many hours of personal prayer, the prayers of our church congregation, and intense psychotherapy all played a role in my personal transformation.

After six or seven months of no contact, Beth Ann and I began dating. We had to start completely over since we did not really know each other. I wanted to be genuine with her, and she wanted to be herself with me. We wanted to communicate without barriers and with nothing held back. I discovered that I really did like Beth Ann, and that she liked me. We now have both love and friendship in our relationship. We are still growing and know that it's not always going to be easy. But thanks to the grace of God we have reconciled and renewed our marriage vows. We have pledged to one another that we will deal with our anger and our wounds daily and never again will we withdraw love and support from one another. We are far stronger than ever before because of God's strength and because of our determination to "hang in there" with one another. We praise God for His great grace to us and for His faithfulness in giving us a new life together.

A WORD TO THE WOMAN

Some women after reading this book or other material on the same topic have breathed a sigh of relief. At least they found a reason for their pain. Many women have sat in my office sobbing with relief that they were not "crazy." Others have been relieved, but then wounded again when they discovered that their pastors, friends, or leaders at their churches did not believe them when they talked about this kind of abuse. They felt betrayed and alone.

Frequently women come burdened by guilt, ashamed that they have lived passively for so long. Some women are ashamed that they have modeled self-defeating patterns for their daughters. Feeling shame and embarrassment is a natural human reaction when we fail. The problem comes when we feel worthless from being who we are (fallible human beings) rather than allowing our shameful behavior to lead to what Scripture calls "repentance without regret" (2 Cor. 7:10, NASB). As children we learned to shame ourselves rather than being ashamed of our behaviors. We associated natural embarrassment with being worthless, rather than allowing ourselves to rejoice in God's grace and freely owning our failures without self-shame. Shame is a feeling of lowered self-esteem; a person recognizes that "I am not all I could, want, or should be." Unfortunately, many of us never learned to handle shame appropriately. In your recovery process, handling shame will be an important task.

Recovery will be a life-long process, so I urge you to let go of any perfectionistic expectations you may have about accomplishing this in a few weeks. With each day that passes you will become more whole. Healing is like an onion—layer after layer is revealed and dealt with—it may seem as if you've "been through this before" but in reality, it is a new layer. Be patient with yourself. You learned to act codependently years ago and it will take a while to get over the humps.

A woman in recovery for six years recently wrote me this letter about her journey to recovery.

SARAH TELLS HER STORY

Five years ago—though I loved the Lord, was in Christian fellowship, and had been baptized in the Holy Spirit—I found myself in an extremity of emotional pain and dysfunction. This was a place in the pit akin to that which the psalmist David cried out to God about; my very life was in the balance. Being a Christian I had a mistrust of secular counseling. Seeing my distress, one of my closest Christian friends located a Christian counselor and with much trepidation I called. Thus began the long journey of unraveling the pieces of my downward spiral. These had been firmly in place since my childhood and I had made many unconscious choices and decisions around them.

My father was a workaholic and while he thought I was very beautiful and was proud of my accomplishments, he was simply not present in my life in terms of shaping my will. He did not hold me accountable or help me set goals. I came into adulthood with these traits largely unformed.

This inner void of which I was unconscious led me into the sin of idolatry for my husband. My reason to exist was to love him, to fit into his life, and make him happy. My unspoken need and motivation was that he made up for the missing parts of myself.

My mother, although very talented in dress design, art, and song writing, was a total caretaker. She was the most loving person I had ever known, and I unconsciously equated caretaking with love. When I became a born-again Christian I used all of the energy of my being to be the total caretaker for my family and to love my husband. I was out of balance and careening toward emotional illness without knowing it. My giving and generous love to others was not balanced with love and care for myself. My generosity and self-sacrificing was not protected with boundaries for myself.

I had reached a point of burnout.

Through counseling, an enormous piece to my puzzle fell into place. My husband was chemically dependent on alcohol. Looking back I can see that the Lord had been trying to get me to seek help in this area five years earlier. I reached a desperate point. I went for a few months to Al-Anon and the children and I even did a loving intervention with my husband. I had chosen before this revelation to live in denial believing Jesus would reach down and heal and save me. I was locked into a deeply destructive pattern similar to what Scripture says: "If a blind man leads a blind man both will fall into the ditch." I was a woman who "loved too much," living with a man whose reality and judgment were being affected by chemical abuse. He had also developed a very subtle way of emotionally abusing me. I was trying to get the affirmation and verbal approval I needed from him, but which he was not going to give me because of his misogyny.

Recovery is for life. Progress—not perfection. I still struggle with feelings of fear and anxiety over things turning out differently than I had planned, but I'm taking responsibility for myself. I am learning to be self-nurturing and am experiencing continual healing through Al-Anon meetings, counseling, and fellowship in my church.

The Lord has worked through counseling to unlock the pieces to my own unconscious choices and even in understanding why I had made them. In Al-Anon, I fulfill the Scripture, "Bear ye one another's burdens and thus fulfill the law of Christ." Here I can work on my fear, perfectionism, and dependent behavior along with others struggling with similar traits. Through the body of Christ I have many loving relationships, and though I love my husband very much, I'm not dependent on a love he is unable to give.

I believe that real demonic spirits come into play in the battle against chemical dependency, codependency, or emotional abuse. Here a knowledge of spiritual warfare and having other Christians to stand and pray with is vitally important in order to break the bonds of the Evil One. Healing does not come through one avenue. The Lord is a practical Lord as well as a Lord of supernatural spiritual power. We must lay down our own preconceived ideas and walk where He asks us to walk in order to be healed. The good news is that the lost time and the suffering, when given back to God, can be used to comfort and encourage others on their journey.

You can begin a journey of healing as this courageous woman has done. The next chapter outlines some of the steps that you will need to undertake.

7

THE WOMAN IN THERAPY AND TREATMENT

This chapter outlines some specific features of the therapy and treatment process for individuals in misogynistic relationships. If you are looking for a therapist to work with you, make sure that they understand these concepts. You might want to suggest that your therapist review this book.

There are certain steps to take to recover from an abusive, misogynistic relationship. The healing process requires commitment, time, and energy. You must get help; you cannot recover alone. Even if your spouse refuses therapy, get professional help for yourself.

THE WOMAN ALONE

Usually the woman seeks help in this type of abusive relationship. The misogynist is happy with things as they are; he likes having the balance of power in his favor and sees no need for help. Often he is eager to see his wife receive therapy because such action only reinforces his belief that "she is the problem, and if she'd stop whining everything would be okay." However, sometimes the man is threatened by the idea of therapy. In these cases the woman usually comes in secret, with a great deal of fear. A woman in this situation may not want to use the family's insurance coverage to pay for therapy, either because she does not want her husband to know or because he has forbidden her to seek help. Occasionally the therapist may be in danger because of the man's great hostility and aversion to treatment.

A therapist must never act shocked or threatened. The woman will interpret this reaction as a sign that she has done the wrong thing by coming in for help or that her case is especially horrible and no one can help her. Protecting the confidentiality of the relationship, even to the extent of not including the woman on the regular office mailing list, is essential. Often I instruct the woman to obtain a post office box in a different community so that she can receive mail without having her husband discover that she is in treatment. Staff members and secretaries must not assume that family members know about treatment; they are not to give out any information. If the therapist consults with a pastor or a church board, those parties must be aware of the importance of confidentiality. Such relationships should be approved in writing by the woman.

When the woman initially comes in alone for therapy and the husband is unwilling to participate, the focus is on the woman. When one family member is in treatment and begins to change, we often see everything begin to change. There is no guarantee that the husband will come in and seek help, but this can happen. At other times the woman changes her behavior sufficiently to protect herself and sets new boundaries for the relationship. The man may not change greatly, but the level of dysfunction in the relationship may be reduced and the woman is safer.

THE STYLE OF THERAPY TO SEEK

If you have decided you are in a misogynistic relationship, then seeking professional help may be your next step; however, it is *crucial* that you find the right kind of counselor. If you choose a counselor who does not understand misogyny, counseling with someone who does not believe that mutual respect is necessary in Christian marrige will do you more harm than good. You might want to consider sharing this book with a potential counselor so you both may discern whether you feel he or she is qualified to deal with the issue of misogyny. Since many therapists have busy schedules, they may not be able to take the time to read an entire book, so I give you my permission as copyright holder to photocopy Appendix E and Figure 1 to share some basic information about misogyny with them. I suggest that you do not share with prospective counselors the details of your personal story until you are confident that they understand the concept of misogyny and mutual submission. If a pastor or Christian counselor does not accept the idea of mutual submission and respect between men and women, then he or she may discount your pain and offer you ineffective therapy. As a consumer seeking help, you have the right to choose your therapist. Just be certain you choose wisely.

If you are a therapist or pastor, you who are trained in nondirective modalities can be uncomfortable dealing with a woman in this type of relationship She is looking for help, action steps, skills, information, and reality-based guidance. She does not want someone to hold her hand, nod empathetically, and say, "My, you seem to be in pain!" She is eager to learn that she is not crazy. The style of therapy needs to be directive, didactic, skills-oriented, cognitively based, and educational. The model we use is based on work by Carkuff,[1] Gazda,[2] and Sweeten.[3] Summarized, the model looks like this:

Stage 1: Build trust and demonstrate caring by using core conditions of empathy, warmth, and respect. Active listening is crucial in this stage in that it frees the woman to tell her story without condemnation.

Stage 2: Maintain the foundation of empathy, warmth, and respect established in Stage 1. Use concreteness, congruence, genuineness, and appropriate self-disclosure to help the woman clarify her needs and goals in therapy, and begin to formulate a plan of action.

Stage 3: Maintain the foundational skills of Stages 1 and 2, thus assuring an open, trusting atmosphere. Encourage the woman to make behavioral changes appropriate to her goals and plan. In this stage the core conditions of confrontation and immediacy come into the foreground.

These stages build upon one another. Rushing to Stage 2 too quickly or skipping over Stages 1 and 2 altogether can be frightening. The woman needs to know that the therapist understands her pain, and cares about and respects her as a person. If a therapist is too matter-of-fact, passive, or spends inadequate time building trust with empathy, warmth, and respect, the woman may assume that this therapist is "like all the other people" who did not understand. Obviously, additional problems will arise if the therapist is male and has misogynistic tendencies of his own.

On the other hand, the therapist must convey that he has seen this type of problem before, understands it well, and has the necessary knowledge and skill to help the woman learn new coping behaviors. A woman in this situation typically believes that she is "the only one" with this type of marital problem and sees herself as a failure, particularly if she is a Christian. She needs reassurance that she is not alone, "crazy," and does not "deserve" the abuse, that there is hope for a better life with or without her spouse.

The therapist can begin to convey this feeling of confidence by active, empathic listening during the first counseling interview. Then, toward the end of the session, the therapist can reply:

"Mary, I have appreciated your candor and courage in coming here to share with me today. I realize that taking this step has been excruciatingly difficult for you. It is embarrassing to tell a total stranger all these intimate details of your life. I hope you can give yourself a pat on the back for taking this step (encourages self-affirmation). I want to share with you some resources and information that will be very helpful and enlightening (sets up positive expectation). First of all, you are not alone. Many other women have experienced the kind of pain that is a part of your life. The confusion and depression you feel is not unusual for a woman in your situation. People who are emotionally or physically abused often feel as you do.

"Second, you can get help to stop the abuse. You can learn to take care of yourself appropriately and set limits with your husband. It is my job to teach you these skills. I have a resource list I will give you (see Appendix C). I want you to go to the library or bookstore and get the book *Christian Men Who Hate Women* or *Can Christians Love Too Much?* by Dr. Margaret Rinck. If you have read these already, please get

Codependent No More by Melody Beattie. You will find these books especially encouraging. See if you can start reading one of them by our next session." (The therapist needs to be specific regarding homework assignments, but also careful not to feed into the codependent's perfectionism and pleaser mentality. Rather than assign specific chapters or number of pages I let individuals read at their own pace. The ideas presented in the books are revolutionary to many women, so they may need to digest them at their own pace.)

This type of closing summary gives a woman the information she needs at that moment, but will not overwhelm her. The bibliotherapy provides an adequate diet of new thoughts and information, and will be self-paced. I also encourage a woman to begin recording thoughts and feelings by maintaining a journal even if she has to keep it at work or with a friend to protect her privacy. This journal becomes an important vehicle through which she can watch her growth.

If there is imminent danger to a woman, either from her own suicidal tendencies or from her husband, steps must be taken to protect her. For one woman in my practice, we had to arrange hospitalization without the husband's knowledge for fear that he would harm her even in the hospital. Legal advice is occasionally necessary, so it is advisable to have a Christian lawyer available who understands abuse. Often a wife is so afraid of offending her husband that she would rather go back into the abusive situation than take protective measures. In such cases the therapist should help the woman assess the risks of such a choice, and then allow her to do so. One of my clients was asked to sign an affidavit acknowledging that we had warned her that her husband was and could continue to be dangerous, and that should he harm her, we were not responsible because we had urged her to protect herself. We took this step after we were certain that the woman was not heeding our warnings about the hazards of her situation.

THERAPY ISSUES VERSUS TREATMENT ISSUES

A woman who relates to a misogynistic man has many issues that need to be addressed in therapy. The woman also needs treatment. Many professionals use the terms "therapy" and "treatment" synonymously; we do not. In our view "treatment" consists of those steps necessary to help a person begin to recover from her codependency. "Therapy" consists of those steps necessary to deal with more all-encompassing root problems in a person's emotional and spiritual life.[4] A woman in a misogynistic relationship is as addicted to that relationship as a heroin addict is to heroin. "Treatment" sets the person on to the road to recovery, so it must precede "therapy." When a codependent comes into the office, the therapist must be aware that until the cycle of relationship addiction to the abusive spouse is broken, the woman will not be "available" or "present" to do the work of therapy. She will remain obsessed with changing her husband or with changing herself so that he will change. While trapped in her codependency, she will not be able to look beyond the pain of the moment to the deeper root causes. Life-and-death patterns are often operating here; thus, the first step is to focus on breaking the addictive cycle.

The goals of the treatment phase are to provide an atmosphere and a process structure so the woman can:

1. stop self-abusive behavior;
2. set limits on abuse by others;
3. understand her own addiction to her misogynistic spouse;

4. understand her own patterns of compulsive behaviors in and out of the relationship, as well as the "triggers" that set her up for acting compulsively;
5. understand what underlying feelings she attempts to avoid or "medicate" by acting codependently;
6. accept both intellectually and emotionally her personal powerlessness and the unmanageability of her life;
7. confront shame and self-blame;
8. work toward new self-definition through taking responsibility for herself in every area of life;
9. come to believe that only a personal relationship to God through Jesus Christ can restore her to sanity (Step 2 of the 12-Step Programs);
10. make a decision to turn her life and her will over to God (Step 3 of 12 Steps);
11. make a fearless moral inventory of her own behavior, thoughts, beliefs, and feelings in every area of life (Step 4);
12. set boundaries to reduce shame when in abusive social or family settings;
13. accept her own personal needs as valid and learn to nurture herself (especially the inner child part of herself) without using codependent patterns;
14. gain intimacy skills and the ability to maintain intimate, meaningful relationships in family and support networks;
15. develop a clear plan for lifelong recovery including therapy, lifestyle changes, career development, and relapse prevention strategies.

Once the treatment phase is accomplished, and the woman is well on the way to recovery, the therapy phase begins. By this time she will have established a peer support network so that when the inevitable conflict arises, she has others to rely on. The therapeutic phase is somewhat less structured than the treatment phase, but is still cognitively and skills oriented. The focus is largely on family of origin issues, other relational issues, inner healing, and emotional work. Because the addictive cycle has been broken and the woman's energy is no longer directed toward obsessions about her husband, she now has energy to focus on her own issues.

The goals of the therapy phase are to create a process/atmosphere/structure such that the woman can

1. maintain a lifestyle free of codependent acting out;
2. grow in interdependence;
3. develop healthy lifestyle skills;
4. learn new coping mechanisms;
5. grow in her Christian community/fellowship;
6. complete her 12-Step work (Steps 6–12);
7. work through family of origin/and abuse issues.

TREATMENT ISSUES

In the treatment phase there are two major steps: assessment and intervention. The major goal of the assessment is to elicit the full story of the misogynistic/codependency relationship from the woman so that she will be able to acknowledge and accept the unmanageability of the situation. Often the codependent is so intensely focused on the spouse's behavior that she cannot see what she may do that maintains the abusive relationship. This statement in no way implies that she deserves the abuse. However, her pattern of learned helplessness has kept the cycle going, and because she can only control her own behavior, we start there.

Particular aspects of any addictive behavior must be addressed in any treatment program.[5] These are: preoccupation, rituals, behavior, unmanageability, emotions, and thinking.

ASSESSMENT

During the assessment step we address these areas as follows:

1. *Preoccupation* What is the woman's addictive cycle? What happens that hooks her into acting out codependently? What happens that hooks her into "acting in"—trying not to do her compulsive, codependent "things" but feeling just as compulsive as ever? What causes her to tolerate misogynistic abuse? How long does a typical misogynistic/codependent cycle of interaction last? How does it end? What does she do to stay focused on her husband after the interaction? What stops the preoccupation? How long until it stops again? With what thoughts, feelings, behaviors is she preoccupied?

2. *Rituals* What rituals (ritualized, repetitive behaviors, actions) does the woman use to maintain the codependency? What does she do that routinely sets her up to act codependently?

3. *Behaviors* What behaviors does the woman engage in when acting out her codependency? Patterns? Types of behavior? Extent? When trying to control her codependency ("acting in")? What triggers set her off to react codependently? How much time does she spend on each behavior?

4. *Unmanageability* What behaviors on her part have gone out of control? What losses has she experienced because of her codependent relationships? How has her codependency affected her life? Her finances? How much time has she lost in focusing on changing her husband (or wishing he'd change)? What toll has her codependency taken on her health? Her

emotions? Her spiritual life? What other compulsive behaviors have developed in her life?

5. *Emotions* What underlying emotions is she "medicating" by remaining codependent? What is her level of depression? Anxiety? Is she suicidal? Does she have manic episodes?

6. *Thinking* Is she demonstrating any psychotic thought patterns? Paranoia? Psychotic thought patterns would include hallucinations, delusions, hearing voices, confused thinking and speech. Paranoia means thinking that people or a group are against you—that they are out to harm you or make you a special object of attention (without an objective basis in fact). What rationalizations does she use to maintain the addiction to her misogynistic partner? What are her core addictive beliefs? In what ways is her thinking distorted? What defense mechanisms does she use? In what way is she in denial? What are the catalytic events or environments that have shaped her beliefs?

These questions are important because people just entering treatment have a lot of denial. Focusing on these questions helps break down the denial.

INTERVENTION

During the intervention step of the treatment phase, we again address these areas:

1. *Preoccupation* Here the therapist teaches the woman the role that preoccupation plays in maintaining her codependency. The concept of the "addictive personality shift" is introduced.[6] The concept is helpful because it allows the woman to distance herself from "the part of her" which is codependent. She can label this her "addict" or her "codependent" self, or whatever term helps her to detach from her compulsive side a bit. We teach a woman that when she is tempted or feels

compelled to do something codependent, she should remember that her personality is shifting gears and that she is starting to listen to her addict again. People in the AA 12-Step Programs use this concept when they say, "That's just my disease talking." This technique helps the woman realize that she has a choice and can say no to the old patterns.

During the preoccupation part of the intervention step, we help the woman grieve the "loss" of her addictive relationship. As Robin Norwood says, these women to some extent become "addicted to excitement."[7] They actually begin to miss the chaos, so we teach them to let go of it and grieve the loss.

Many women have never known anything but chaos interpersonally, so this change is quite traumatic.

We also begin to teach a woman new coping mechanisms to deal with anxiety. In the past she used codependent behaviors to stifle her fears. Now she needs new methods such as meditation on Scripture, journal writing, and relaxation exercises. The next step helps the woman become aware of her personal limits and vulnerabilities. No matter how weak they feel, codependents demand too much of themselves. They are rigidly perfectionistic and have a difficult time accepting their personal fallibility without irrational self-blame.

2. *Rituals* First we place an injunction on rituals. Then we replace old rituals with new ones. For example, we encourage a woman to find a sponsor or mentor and encourage practices such as 12-Step meetings; use of journals to record her thoughts and feelings; and use of workbooks for personal growth. Next we set a date for stopping codependent behaviors. The following step is to regularly recognize progress by encouraging her to celebrate it symbolically; for example, by means of self-rewards, group celebration, or group recognition.

3. *Behaviors* Here we contract with the woman regarding limits on her codependent behaviors. We also provide training in new coping behaviors and assist her in establishing codependent "sobriety." For example, Shirley had been dating Hank, an alcoholic. He was verbally abusive to her, but Shirley knew how much Hank needed her. However, she realized that the relationship could be destructive, so she contracted to call a friend whenever she recognized in herself a codependent, rescuing response, such as bailing Hank out of jail or lending him money. Then she could discuss her feelings and potential actions.

4. *Unmanageability* In this step we use the uncovered unmanageability as a lever to contract for change. We initiate second-order change to disrupt the system (e.g., paradoxical intention, ordeal therapy), helping the woman to be honest about feelings and thinking. We reinforce Step 1, regarding unmanageability, when denial returns and help her to accept her human imperfections and her need for help from others (Step 4). We guide her through Steps 2 and 3 regarding accepting help from God, and we help her learn how to assess her susceptibility to relapse.

5. *Emotions* Here we arrange for appropriate medication, if necessary, to manage depression. We also remain open to hospitalization, if necessary. We teach the ABCs of Emotions, and the Five Rules of Rational Thinking and Feeling.[8] We also teach the role of shame and guilt in recovery, and establish relapse prevention strategies.

6. *Thinking* Here we confront gross defenses and work to help the woman accept the situation. We encourage her to confront impaired or distorted thinking. We also teach her feedback mechanisms to help her keep reality in focus, and assign her a task (e.g., writing out her "secrets" list) to help her deal with any shame. These steps are not necessarily done

in this order. They may overlap one another. The point is that all of these areas are addressed.

THERAPY

Reclamation

There are two phases to therapy: reclamation and reentry. The goal of the reclamation phase is for the woman to systematically review her life and relationships in order to rebuild her life and reclaim lost parts. Codependents have experienced many losses; grieving these losses and reclaiming lost parts of themselves becomes an important part of their therapy.[9] Thus, family-of-origin work is essential during reclamation.

There are three parts to family-of-origin work: Examining the family influence, examining the woman's own contribution, and healing the wounds from the past.

We describe these areas as separate, but in practice they tend to overlap. However, it is important for the clinician to know whether all these areas are covered over the course of therapy. Generally, the woman's own needs set the pace in this phase, but the therapist needs to steadily guide the woman so that all these crucial areas are covered.

The Family Influence When we examine a family problem or a dysfunctional marital relationship, we frequently find generational problems below the surface. Patterns learned from watching parents and grandparents become unconscious cognitive road maps for present-day scenarios. Bowen and other family systems therapists stress the importance of intergenerational patterns in family or marital therapy.[10]

Use of a genogram reveals patterns of family functioning,

relationships, and structure continuing from one generation to another.[11] Constructing a genogram or family tree is an eye-opening experience for a woman (see figure 5). As she becomes aware of the generational nature of the dysfunction in her family-of-origin, she realizes she is not alone; others in her family have also operated dysfunctionally.

We help a woman examine generational patterns of abuse (emotional, physical, sexual), alcoholism and/or chemical addiction, and compulsive behaviors (codependency, overeating, workaholism, anorexia or bulimia, gambling, sexual addiction). Once she sees that others in the family were codependent or compulsive, she can stop shaming herself for having learned this pattern. On a spiritual level, seeing these patterns helps in knowing how to pray to cut the spiritual ties to dysfunction ("law of generations"). At this point in therapy, we encourage the woman to review Step 1 of the 12-Step Workbook in order to admit her life is unmanageable. (A number of fine workbooks are available. We recommend beginning with *A Gentle Way Through the 12 Steps.*)[12] By reviewing the first step, the woman can go back and closely examine the amount of powerlessness she experiences because of family-of-origin patterns learned in childhood. If she has not completed a genogram already, we make the assignment. We also go through the abuse checklist and addiction interaction sections of Step 1 in *A Gentle Way.*

At this point another helpful project is having the woman draw a life-map from birth to the present (see figure 6, p. 145). One anorectic woman did this early in her therapy. She was stunned to see the amount of trauma she had experienced in twenty-five years. She had never faced all the crisis events at once and their relationship to the development of her eating disorder. This graphic exercise often proves the old adage "a picture is worth a thousand words."

FIGURE 5 – GENOGRAM EXERCISE

FAMILY NAME _____   DATE _____

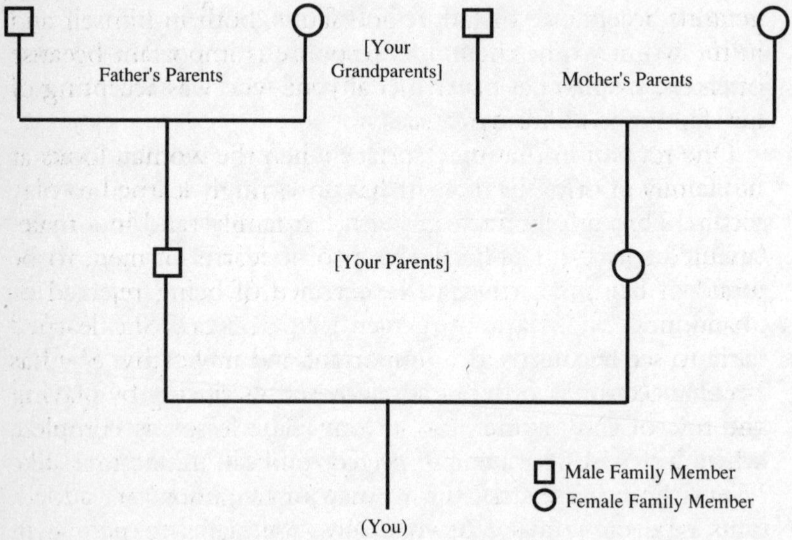

[Your Grandparents]

Father's Parents   Mother's Parents

[Your Parents]

☐ Male Family Member
○ Female Family Member

(You)

A genogram is a way of charting the relationships in your family tree. Understanding family history helps us to understand the power of dsyfunctional misogynistic relationships and addictions in our lives. Diagram your family tree for 3 generations. Use the codes below to categorize each family member.

Codes:

1. Alcoholic
2. Compulsive gambler
3. Anorectic/bulimic
4. Compulsive overeater

5. Sex addict
6. Victim of child abuse
7. Perpetrator of child abuse
8. Mental health problem

9. Codependent
10. Other compulsive disorders
11. Misogynist
12. Other problems/issues

©1990 Margaret Josephson Rinck

130

The Woman's Own Contribution The second part of reclamation in therapy is examining the role of the woman's own
behavior in her situation. This phase is often quite painful,
since she has been taught to shame herself severely for any
"bad" behavior or minor "faults." The therapist must model
genuine acceptance of failure and faults, both in himself and
in the woman. The therapist's response is important because
often the woman has never met anyone who was accepting of
her failures and idiosyncrasies.

One revelation that may surface when the woman looks at
her family of origin is that she has unwittingly learned to play
victim. Through interactions with her family (and in a male-
oriented society), she has learned to be fearful of men, to be
afraid of being assertive, to be terrified of being rejected or
abandoned by anyone—by men in particular. She learned
early to see her needs as unimportant and unworthy. She has
become accustomed to being overly self-sacrificing by playing
the role of the placater for so long. The lesson is complete
when a few often misinterpreted biblical injunctions like
"Turn the other cheek" or "Love your neighbor" are added.
This type of woman automatically capitulates to people in
authority; it never occurs to her to be assertive or to question.
(However, this capitulation may not be true in every area of
her life. Some women married to misogynists are assertive
professionals outside the home, but find that their backbones
turn to jelly in personal relationships.)

Women who marry misogynists (and other codependent
women) usually give unconscious "signals," which allow
other people to bully them.[13] These learned signals are
unconscious things a woman does that facilitate the abuse.
Acknowledging these contributing patterns in no way excuses
the man for being abusive, and should not be interpreted as
reasons for "blaming the victim." Codependency being what

it is, we must look at all contributions to the "sick" system in our search for truth.

What are some learned signals that set up a woman for abuse or allow it to continue? Let's examine a few.

1. *Always assuming that the other person is right, and its corollary, always accepting the blame even when it is inappropriate to do so.* Most codependents, whether male or female, identify with this trait. Children from dysfunctional families often learn to take the blame as a way of placating an irate sibling or parent. Sometimes a desire to rescue a sibling from trouble encourages the person to say "I did it" and take the beating for the other child. This pattern of always taking the "one down" position, always feeling wrong, always assuming that others know better than oneself, molds one into a compliant, obedient, fearful, mindless creature. The ability to think, question, react, or even feel is lost. Rather than reacting out of her adult side, this woman responds from her helpless child side. For example:

Husband: (questioning and berating his wife for a decision she made) "Why did you do that?"

Wife: (from child position—stammering and looking downcast) "Well, I don't know! I just did it. I thought it was best. . . ."

Wife: (alternative adult response) "I can see you question my decision. Tell me what you think was wrong with it."

2. *Using a tentative communication style:* qualifying remarks ("I think we should . . ." or "Perhaps I . . ." or "I may be wrong, but . . ."); beating around the bush (repeating herself obsessively); never getting to the point; being vague about what

she really wants or feels. An example of this style is the following exchange:

Wife: "It's really nice out tonight."

Husband: "Uh huh."

Wife: "Saw the Smiths taking a walk a few minutes ago. They seemed to be enjoying the coolness."

Husband: "Oh."

Wife: "The leaves sure look pretty."

Husband: "Look, will you please quit pestering me. Can't you see I am reading the paper?"

Obviously, the wife wanted to go for a walk with her husband in this example. Instead of being direct about her needs, she was indirect. A person using this communication style does so out of fear of rejection and a fear of taking responsibility for her own words and feelings. Unconsciously she scares herself with thoughts such as, "What if he doesn't want to go for a walk with me? I'd feel so rejected. I couldn't stand it." Or, "What if he thinks I am sentimental for wanting to go out and enjoy the fall colors? I couldn't stand for him to think I am sentimental or stupid!"

3. *"Dumping": giving others too much information which can easily be used against oneself.* Overexplaining, inappropriate self-disclosure, and talking too much fall into this category. The idea behind this behavior is "If I talk enough and keep up a stream of words, I'll ward off any harm (and/or I'll keep him from leaving me)." For a woman who uses this behavior, silence means rejection or impending doom, so she tries to fill the silence. However, she often sets herself up for the very thing she fears. Take the example of the woman who looks into her husband's tool chest and notices that the small

133

needle-nose pliers is missing. She doesn't need it, and knows that her husband's pattern is to raise a ruckus and blame her when tools are missing, but she blurts out compulsively, "Oh, my! Your needle-nose pliers is missing." She could have taken out what she needed, set the lid down quickly, and walked away. Instead she feels compelled to comment on the fact that the pliers is missing. Of course, true to form, her husband raises a ruckus and blames her.

4. *Rescuing or excusing others: justifying other people's unacceptable behavior by making excuses for them.* This pattern is common among women married to misogynists. They seem to have a compulsive need to get others off the hook—and to blame themselves! By excusing the behavior of others, they can push it away along with their own feelings of pain, anger, fear, or rejection. For example, "Well, I know he only hit her because he was drunk. He really loves our daughter." Or, "If he weren't working so hard, he'd have more patience and would not lose his temper." Or, "But that isn't the real him. He's just feeling so much pressure right now."

5. *Highlighting one's own weaknesses; that is, attacking oneself before someone else does.* Self-esteem and self-confidence are so low in these women that they feel safer if they beat up themselves emotionally than if others do. Example: You arrive unexpectedly at your friend's home. Although the house looks all right to you, she apologizes for "the mess," pointing out the dust and soda glasses on the end tables.

6. *Nonverbal cues: timid or unassertive body language; frightened facial expression; wimpy or sickeningly sweet tone of voice; self-deprecatory gestures; nonassertive or self-humiliating actions.* A woman who rarely, if ever, makes eye contact with other adults; a wife who turns her head or looks away from others when they speak; a young woman with a singsong, cheerful lilt to her voice even when she is talking about her older

brother slapping her across the face are examples of this nonverbal behavior that exacerbates or at least reinforces abuse.

Healing the Wounds from the Past The third element of family-of-origin work helps the woman mourn the past, receive some measure of healing, and learn new skills for healthier living.

Many, if not all, of a woman's behaviors that contribute to an abusive pattern in her marriage were learned long before she met her husband. Codependent behavior does not spring "full-blown from the head of Zeus." It develops early in life, and explains why some partners are attractive while others are not. Unfortunately, it is the misogynist or the "needy" man whom most codependent women find attractive.[14] Often *repetition compulsion* is an element in the choosing of a partner: the woman unconsciously tries to repeat an old familial pattern through old ways of behaving, hoping to win over the "unavailable" or "unloving" man this time (because she failed to win Daddy over as a child).

As Judith Viorst says so well:

In repeating painful experience we are refusing to lay to rest our childhood ghosts. We continue to clamor for something that cannot be. No matter how hard they clap for us now, she will never clap for us then. We have to relinquish that hope. We have to let go. For we cannot climb into a time machine, become that long gone child and get what we want when we oh so desperately wanted it. The days for that getting are over, finished, done. We have needs we can meet in different ways, in better ways, in ways that create new experience. But until we can mourn that past, until we can mourn and let go of that past, we are doomed to repeat it.[15]

Much of this process does not occur in neat, concise, preprogrammed steps, but there is a flow to it. We can discern certain elements that help facilitate growth. These steps apply to both the woman and man caught in a misogynistic relationship. Up to this point we have focused on the woman alone, because usually the misogynistic male is not the first to call for an appointment. Some unique considerations must be addressed in dealing with the male partner of the relationship. These will be addressed in the next chapter.

8

THE MISOGYNIST IN THERAPY AND TREATMENT

As mentioned earlier, in a misogynistic relationship it is usually the woman who seeks help. Unfortunately, the man is content with things the way they are and is too eager to conceptualize the problem as his wife "needing to see a shrink."

Even when a couple seeks help together, a therapist must work separately with the woman for a while. The reason is that the woman is frequently emotionally distraught and has incredibly low self-esteem by the time she comes in for help. She is often *convinced* that *she* is the "sick" one and that everything would be fine in the marriage if she could just control *herself*. She does not see the marriage relationship as sick because the misogynist has convinced her that she is crazy.

Work with the couple truly begins after the woman is stabilized, educated about the real problem (the marriage relationship), and feels better about herself. Both partners will need to change if the relationship is to become viable.

WHY HE RESISTS

Usually a misogynist is extremely resistant to treatment. Denial is so great that drastic measures are necessary in order to gain his attention. Very often the only reason he comes in is because his wife says she will leave him if he does not or she has left him already.

The misogynist believes there is nothing wrong with the marriage. He truly believes that "everything" would be fine if his wife would just do what he asks. Even when he has had an affair, he blames it on his wife because she is "frigid" or "unloving." He has no idea that he is the one who is cold and unfeeling. The feelings that normally motivate change— sadness, guilt, remorse, anxiety—are not a significant part of his emotional experience.[1] He is not hurting enough to seek help unless a crisis is precipitated; even if it is, he often divorces his wife and finds a girlfriend before enough time has elapsed for the pain to set in. If he does come to therapy, his goal is to see that the therapist "fixes" his partner. The misogynist sees therapy as a threat to his control and manipulation in the relationship and in the home. Whenever the therapist tries to focus on him, his feelings, his part of the relationship, he deflects the focus with a barrage of jokes, charm, words, and stories. He often drops out of therapy and pursues divorce because he is unable to face himself.

It is sad, but the reality is that very few misogynists accept treatment. Most would rather risk losing their spouse than risk opening up. Such relationships do not change unless both people are willing to work together.

THE ROLE OF THE CHURCH IN MAINTAINING DENIAL

The problem is compounded when the church reinforces the abuse. Sometimes the pastor and the elders and misconstrued biblical theology can bolster the misogynist's denial as illustrated in Mary's case (see chapter 1). Mary's husband told the pastor that the reason why he beat their oldest child, punched and brutalized his wife, and forced her to engage in sadomasochistic sexual rituals was that she "was not submissive enough." The horror is that the pastor and the elders, all graduate school or college-educated, believed him! Even the church-appointed psychiatrist reportedly told her that her husband did these things because she was not a virgin when they married (he had seduced her). The church elders and the pastor set up a list of rules for her to follow, and made her agree not to leave her home for more than five hours per week! This "discipline" was not leveled against a slovenly housekeeper who neglected her family but against a woman who kept a beautiful home (despite six young children) and who was attractive, a good cook, and a people pleaser. Yet the pastor and the elders continued to blame her, even when it was evident that the children were being scarred emotionally! They even forbade her to seek psychological help for her children. The fact that she was able to reach out for help against their pressures, as passive, dependent, and people-pleasing as she was, is a miracle in itself!

ONCE IN THERAPY

If a misogynist comes in for therapy, I have found that it is important to get him into a therapy group for men with the same problem. If it is labeled as a group for "men who hate women," they will not go, so I describe it as "a therapy group for men who *feel* that they give and give and whose wives respond with anger." This expression describes how *they* see themselves and their situation, so they usually accept it. I work with the couple while the husband is in the group, and see the wife individually and/or in a women's group.

It is gratifying to see healing when it does occur, especially because it is so rare. Sometimes I recommend "a covenant separation," whereby the couple lives separately for six to nine months while seeing each other only in my office (at first). Later, as things progress, they begin "dating" again and start to rebuild a relationship. The goal is not separation leading to divorce, but covenanting to separate so as to reunite. This separation period gives them a breather and a chance to let some wounds heal without being ripped open again.

Even with this format, the process is slow and laborious. With one couple, fourteen months of therapy were needed before the man gained sufficient strength and insight to see his controlling behavior for what it was. In the meantime, his wife was hospitalized for anxiety and depression, his children stopped talking to him, and things became more chaotic both in and out of therapy.

In another case the husband never was able to see his dysfunctional role in the marriage, although he and his wife were in therapy for over a year during their separation. Eventually she filed for divorce, and he felt deeply threatened. However, instead of opening up and dealing with his fear of abandonment, he (like many misogynists) had an affair, got engaged, and thereby cut himself off from the opportunity to deal with his own root issues.

Thus, even in a Christian context, the prognosis for repairing a misogynistic marriage is not very good. These types of men tend to use God, the church, and the Bible as they use everything else—to bolster their worldview. No one sees the broken, hurt little boy underneath the bravado, least of all the misogynist himself. Occasionally a misogynist will be courageous enough not to replace his wife so quickly with another woman; the pain will surface and he will break through to healing. Even so, the road back is painful and time-consuming. Trust has to be rebuilt slowly, and both partners must learn to deal with their own issues in the relationship. If healing is to occur, both partners need to face their deep fear of abandonment and their need to control. Both must learn to be more honest with feelings (often discovering what their feelings *are*). Each will need to learn to communicate those feelings without blaming, without power plays, and with kindness. Old patterns die hard, and these types of relationships take a long time to heal.

9

THE STEPS TO RECOVERY

HEALING THE SHAME AND FEAR OF ABANDONMENT

After a therapeutic alliance has been established between the misogynist and his wife, their therapy program will entail the following elements.

BEGINNING AGAIN

The power of shame and fear comes from the silence that surrounds a couple and the other people involved. As long as we keep quiet and do not "name the monster," it continues to have power over us. The more time we spend in silence, the more that shame and fear powerfully bind us to the past.

John Bradshaw in his book *Healing the Shame That Binds You*[1] goes into great detail on this subject, as do Merle A.

Fossum and Marilyn J. Mason in their book *Facing Shame: Families in Recovery*.[2] These books were not written from an evangelical perspective, but both contain important concepts about shame, fear, and recovery. These authors and others reinforce the biblical principle of confession (i.e., breaking the silence). As pastors, counselors, and therapists, we must help people open up, face their shame and fear, and grow beyond it. The old adage "confession is good for the soul" is still true. We see it at work at the beginning of every 12-Step based recovery meeting. A person stands and says "Hi. I'm . . . and I am a recovering . . ." Confession—it works.

Many people are afraid to own up to the shame and fear that plagues them, especially to a pastor or other authority figure. We must create an atmosphere where someone can feel safe enough to confess without fear of rejection.

There is no one way of approaching this subject, but there seems to be certain milestones a person needs to cover in order to recover fully. Some of these markers are internal (within the person) and others are behavioral (external). Figure 5 outlines these markers or milestones. Inner milestones are primarily decisions or acts of the will that the person makes. Outer milestones are the corresponding behavioral changes a person makes. For example, internally, the person decides to stop shaming herself, commits to uncovering her secrets, and renounces the old patterns of self-blame. In order to carry these decisions out externally, she begins to share her secrets with various safe people. She makes a "Secret Shame List" and crosses off items as they are confessed.

A therapist or pastor slowly guides the person through these milestones, realizing that each individual's pace of recovery and restoration is different. These milestones need not be experienced in the order listed. Some may come simultaneously or in phases. For example, some people begin

FIGURE 6 — A LIFE MAP

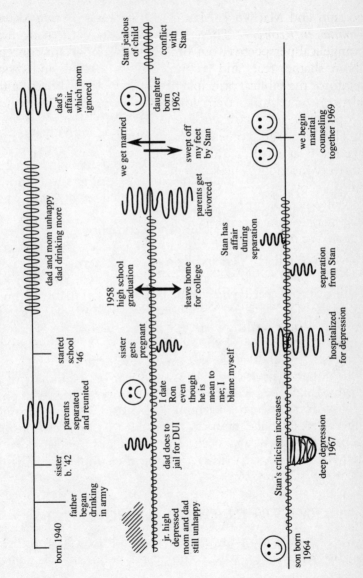

born 1940

father began drinking in army

sister b. '42

started school '46

parents separated and reunited

dad and mom unhappy dad drinking more

dad's affair, which mom ignored

Stan jealous of child

conflict with Stan

we get married

daughter born 1962

swept off my feet by Stan

parents get divorced

1958 high school graduation

leave home for college

sister gets pregnant

dad does to jail for DUI

jr. high depressed mom and dad still unhappy

I date Ron even though he is mean to me; I blame myself

Stan has affair during separation

separation from Stan

hospitalized for depression

we begin marital counseling together 1969

Stan's criticism increases

deep depression 1967

son born 1964

©1990 Margaret Josephson Rinck

to heal their shame and fear by developing awareness and coming alive inside. Others start with the decision to stop shaming themselves, since they are already aware that they do it. Making a decision to stop shaming oneself seems easy when examined superficially. However, the therapist or pastor must be continually aware of the difficulty a person faces in this process. It is one thing to say "Just make a decision to. . . ." and another to actually do it. Some individuals come from such disturbed backgrounds that they are unaware that there even is a choice. Most people need to first learn the differences between shame and guilt. For others, the knowledge that someone was trying to put their own shame onto them as children, freezes them up.

These milestones are not easily accomplished 1-2-3 steps. For any changes to last the inner work is necessary. However, many times when a person begins to act (externally) in a new way, the inner work is more quickly completed. Sometimes it is difficult to discern which came first—the action or the inner decision. In some ways it does not matter. Both elements are necessary for a healthy recovery and restoration. A therapist will be able to discover the "warp and woof" of the garment being woven and guide the process accordingly.

Healing the underlying shame and fear of abandonment is at the base of the recovery/restoration process. The re-parenting process, which both (the misogynist and his wife) must undergo, is crucial. The roots of the misogynistic relationship go back into early life. We must understand the elements of the healing process in order to bring the couple (or individual) to wholeness.

ELEMENTS IN THE HEALING PROCESS

The therapist must use utmost skill and dedication to help the husband and/or wife combine the following elements.

FIGURE 7

HEALING SHAME
AND FEAR OF ABANDONMENT

INNER RESOLVE (INTERNAL DECISION)	OUTER ACTION (BEHAVIORAL)
Decide to give up shaming yourself. Commit to uncovering your secrets. Renounce patterns of self-blame.	Talk about the secrets (Break the No-Talk Rule). - Secret Shame List - Confession Principle - 12 Step Group - Sponsor - Pastor, Therapist
Renew your mind. Change your thoughts regarding: - Self - Others - God - Situations	Act Assertively. - Act, don't react - Know what you think and feel - "Say - Ask" Formula (say what you need first, then ask your question)
Come alive, develop awareness, refuse to merely "go through the motions".	Notice your body (How does it look, feel, smell, talk, sit?). Notice your feelings and thoughts. Be alert for positive things around you; list fifteen positive items a day. Pay attention to the environment, keep a journal and record what you notice.
Decide to accept yourself as you are. Reject driving yourself to be perfect. Give yourself permission to be human. Forgive yourself for failures.	Act lovingly toward yourself by - Disciplining yourself - Delaying gratification appropriately - Resting, relaxing, having fun - Meeting your needs in healthy ways - Developing a balanced lifestyle - Parenting yourself
Commit to always "being there" for your inner child.	Get a photo of yourself when you were less than five years old. Frame and place it where you will see it often. Talk regularly to the child and reassure him that you "are there" for him.
Set your will to protect yourself, help yourself love, forgive, and accept yourself in healthy ways.	Thought-stopping, new self-talk, and healthy distraction techniques to reprogram patterns of self-hate, unforgiveness, rejection of self.
Determine to strengthen your ability to use the support resources that are available to you, within and without yourself. Commit to Jesus Christ as your "Ultimate Support Person."	List your resources on paper. Example: God's Word, church, best friend, sibling, counseling, school, work, career guidance, relatives, friends, small groups, etc.

1. Unremitting honesty in self-examination. Couples must take the focus off each other and focus on their inner self. "Lord, change me!" must become their heart's cry. At times gentle confrontation is needed to prod them into dropping their defenses and looking at their own behaviors. Denial was a defense that helped them to survive a horrible situation; now they need to let it go.

2. Courage to acknowledge, listen to, and love the little child within their personality. Jesus said that we cannot enter the kingdom except as little children; yet, both the misogynist and his wife are fearful of their inner child. Many have been running away from this child. Others despise and hate the child within, seeing it as "weak," "stupid," "a sissy," a "baby." Still others view their inner child as shameful or are afraid to feel the pain. They fear that if the pain ever came out, it would overwhelm and destroy them.

Both the misogynist and his wife keep the child locked up, hidden in the basement of their mind and heart. One way to help them begin to love their inner child is to ask them to find a childhood photo of themselves. Then they can learn to speak with that inner child of long ago. Role playing helps make such a dialogue come alive; so does the empty chair technique, where they imagine their inner child in the chair. Others carry the photo with them daily. Some frame it and give it a place of honor on their desk. In holding a dialogue with the child, they can ask the following questions:

What was it like growing up in our family?

How did you feel when . . .

Dad drank?

Mom cried?

Grandpa died?

Sister hit you?

Why do you think I am afraid of . . .

women?

men?

God?

children?

failure?

success?

Why am I a compulsive . . .

overeater?

gambler?

drinker?

workaholic?

religious worker?

sports fiend?

What do you need as my inner child? What can I give you that will help you feel safe?

I encourage both the misogynist and his wife to conduct these dialogues out loud and/or in writing. It is amazing to see what kind of information surfaces when they allow themselves the freedom to know this long-hidden part of themselves.

3. Steadfastness in the effort to "grow up." Ironically, while stuffing their hurting inner child into a closet, these couples often allowed the rebellious child to come out and wreak havoc. Sometimes this rebellion *looks* rebellious; at other times it looks whiny, sulky, and full of pouting behavior. Behind both types of rebellion lies the desire to control others. In a misogynistic relationship both partners suffer from this problem. The wife tries to control the husband by alternately being sweet, long-suffering, patient, kind, obedient, passive, helpful, caring, and dutiful and being sad, tearful, pouting, hurt, devastated, crushed, humiliated, and terrified. The husband tries to control the wife by keeping her off balance. One minute he's sweet, charming, kind, and adoring. The next he's tyrannical, screaming (or silent), mean, and selfish. *Both* partners are terrified of abandonment. *Neither* is successful at controlling the other.

"Growing up," then, involves giving up control. Contrary to the myth that becoming an adult means you can have all the control you want, these couples need to learn that to gain control they must "lose it" (a summary of Jesus' teaching). By discovering that they are "helpless," they are free to turn over control to God and to be (as AA puts it) "Restored to sanity" (Steps 1–12).

This process of growing up involves leaving behind Peter Pan and Never-Never Land. It means facing reality and life as it is now, taking responsibility for one's own behavior, and letting go of control over others. "Growing up" means accepting that "life ain't fair" and that "life is difficult."[3] The "Serenity Prayer" becomes a daily practice not for piety's sake, but for the sake of sanity.

4. Re-parenting oneself is a lifelong process. Part of "growing up" becomes the task of redeeming the past by re-parenting oneself. Those dependency needs that went unmet by parents must be fulfilled by the child, the new adult.

The misogynist and his wife must acknowledge that because they did not always receive what they needed as children, and because they cannot go back in time to relive those events, they are now responsible for reaching out for the "substantial healing" available to them this side of eternity.[4] Therapists, pastors, and friends can help in the re-parenting process, but no one can do it completely for another person. Individuals must take responsibility for their own healing.

How can couples begin to re-parent themselves? *First, they must face their old anger about not receiving what they needed.* Many couples (men in particular) find this difficult. They excuse, explain, and justify parental behavior, by using their adult reasoning to deny childhood pain. The therapist must help them slowly peel away at layers of denial until the memories of neglect, hurt, and abuse reconnect with the feelings of rage, terror, and pain.

Second, they must forgive their parents. John and Paula Sandford, Matthew and Dennis Linn, and Lewis Smedes all provide excellent help in this area (see Resource List). The key is helping the individual to see that forgiveness is a process. Many people are impatient and want to skip from "I hate you" to "I forgive you" without the appropriate emotional work between the two.

Third, they must forgive themselves and ask for God's forgiveness for wrong doing. In this area Steps 4 and 5 of the 12 Steps are very helpful. There are numerous workbooks to guide a person through a "searching and fearless moral inventory" (see Resource List). My first recommendation is *A Gentle Way Through the 12 Steps* by Patrick Carnes and *The Twelve Steps: A Spiritual Journey* by Recovery Publications. The fourth step in these workbooks helps people to see both positive and negative elements in their moral development. It also focuses on helping them release shame, anger, fear, sadness, loneliness, and discomfort—feelings that contribute to the grieving process discussed in the fourth and fifth steps.

Following through with Steps 6–12 will continue the healing and re-parenting process.

Fourth, couples must renew their minds or reprogram their mental computers. It is impossible to review the basic cognitive therapy processes here, but I want to suggest a few helpful techniques. Using affirmations and biblical quotations can be extremely useful in changing old thought patterns. I encourage couples to read some of the many statements available in books, but to also write their own. Some record their own versions on tape and listen to them while dressing or driving to work. Writing "coping dialogues" is helpful, especially for those who have trouble imagining themselves following new behaviors flawlessly.[5] By writing a self-dialogue in which they see themselves *coping* with the new situation rather than *mastering* it perfectly, they learn to affirm themselves even in the midst of less-than-perfect performance.

Another crucial element is renewing one's mind about one's view of God. Many individuals see God as an extension of an abusive father. They find themselves alienated emotionally from the "love of God" by projecting onto the heavenly Father all the characteristics of their abusive, or neglectful, or absent earthly father. The Sandfords and others have dealt with this subject extensively, so I will only mention it here. (See Resource List).

Fifth, in re-parenting, the misogynist and his wife must identify the type of skills (or lack thereof) that they saw modeled in their families, and then strengthen their own self-nurturing skills. Writing a "mothering" or "fathering" script describing what they remember as children is helpful. Observing their own parenting style can also be instructive. After deciding what they want to change, couples can replace old habits with new ones such as, the use of "thought stopping" to halt old, destructive self-talk patterns; reciting positive Bible verses to counter old, negative messages; writing a letter to their inner child promising not to shame her anymore for not being perfect; giving themselves permission to be fallible human beings; doing something nice for themselves at least once a day; beginning to ask for what they need; listening to their bodies: resting when tired, eating when hungry.

After re-parenting, the next stage of healing the wounds from the past involves prayer and what some people call "inner healing." It is beyond the scope of this book to deal extensively with prayer and healing in therapy, but many articles, books, and other resources are available. Suffice it to say that Scripture commands us to pray for the sick (James 5). I believe that this command includes those sick in mind, spirit, and heart as well as in body. There are some things that only God can accomplish. We can work with people by talking, teaching, and giving them skills, but only God can provide the grace they need to forgive. The problem of evil is confronted daily by therapists. What one being can do and has done to another are representations of evil incarnate. As therapists we also need prayer. James 5:15 instructs us to pray for the one who is ill, and "the Lord will raise him up." We can empathize, counsel, pray, cajole, and confront, but only God can "raise them up." If we take on the burden, we too will become burdened down. Prayer releases the person to God, putting the situation in His hands, not in ours. Through prayer, we open a door of grace and make a way for others to experience God's supernatural power.

However, prayer is not magic. Prayers are not always answered in the way we expect. Sometimes there appears to be no answer, only silence. Then we must remain steadfast models like Job: "Though he slay me, yet will I hope in him" (Job 13:15). The misogynist and his wife need to see faith modeled in good times and bad times, in "easy" times and difficult times. Sometimes prayers seem unanswered until months later when we look back and clearly "see" the unseen hand of God at work. We must grow daily in our own walk with Christ to model grace and faith. We must "work our program of recovery," as they say in AA. We cannot pass on to others that which we do not possess. Personal prayer, meditation, and study of the Word are essential parts of a Christian therapist's regimen.

I recall a thirty-year-old woman who came to me for counseling some years ago. She had come from a dysfunctional family, losing one family member to suicide and another to a tragic accident. One of her parents had recently died in another city after a long illness. She had been a Christian for four or five years, having previously led a rather loose and free-wheeling life. She was depressed and guilt-ridden over the many affairs and liaisons she had had both before and after meeting the Lord. It had taken her some time to understand why Scripture calls for chastity before marriage. At the time she saw me she was living a chaste life, but was still burdened by guilt.

In this situation, as in others, I encouraged her to examine her past sexual experiences. She came to the next session with a list of at least fifty names. She was humbled deeply by realizing the extent of her past promiscuity; she had never faced it all at once until that day. She remembered some of the people clearly; in other cases she could remember only the place, the setting, or the man's face. Yet all were seared deeply into her conscience. The shame she felt was overwhelming.

We took her list, name by name, situation by situation, to the Lord and we prayed. She prayed for forgiveness for her own "inappropriate sexual involvement" (without going into all the ugly details). Speaking forgiveness to each one who had defrauded her sexually, as if he were there, she said, "So and so, I forgive you for your inappropriate sexual involvement with me." Then I claimed Scriptures regarding confession and forgiveness, and prayed for God's Spirit "to separate her from this person and from anything that came to her emotionally, physically, spiritually, or mentally as a result of that relationship." After we had gone through the whole list—a process that filled a number of sessions—I prayed for deep inner healing and a filling of her "empty rooms," where so much pain had been, with the warm light of God's love. I prayed that God would fill her with joy in being a sexual person, and would free her to be all that He created her to be. After that last prayer session, she reported that she felt "as if 100 pounds had been lifted off of my back." We continued to work together for a while on other issues, and she terminated. A year or two later on her wedding day, she whispered in my ear, "I'm so happy! I feel just like a virgin!" God had indeed restored "the years that the locust have eaten" (Joel 2:25).

In relation to a misogynistic marriage relationship, I think of a married woman in her fifties who came to me because of depression. It turned out that her husband was both an alcoholic and a misogynist. We worked together for a long time, and prayer was an integral part of the therapy. At one point in the therapy we were in prayer about her home and her relationship to her husband. She had become too afraid and too tense to be in the house for long periods of time, even when her husband was not at home. In prayer, the Lord gave me a clear impression of demonic harassment there—in fact, a spirit of death. It was as if her home itself was oppressed or burdened. So I prayed with her. We rebuked Satan in Jesus' name, and with His authority, by faith, broke the power of that spirit of death. Immediately upon arriving home that afternoon she noticed that the feeling of oppression was gone, and that the house itself seemed lighter. Even her children (who are not Christians and did not know of the prayer) said it seemed different! Although her husband was still drinking and acting cruelly toward her, winning that spiritual battle in prayer gave her the strength to continue.

I could give numerous examples of the effect of prayer in therapy, but the main point is to recognize that Jesus Christ is alive and that His power is available to us when we pray. There are times when only God's Spirit can sufficiently release a person from pain and bitterness so that they are enabled to forgive a spouse—whether misogynistic or otherwise! Only God can help people face their deepest fears of abandonment, give up games of control and manipulation, and grow toward intimacy. We must be open to God's power in these areas.

In summary, we have seen that the first part of the process involves "reclamation"—helping both the misogynist and his wife reclaim or redeem new hope for the future out of their broken pasts.

REENTRY

The second part of the therapy process, after reclamation, is reentry. Reentry involves a number of objectives; the first objective is to help the individual develop an "after-therapy plan." This plan should include but not be limited to the following:

1. Written, manageable, concrete goals for one month, two months, four months, six months, nine months, and twelve months in each of the areas where the individual needs to continue working.

Example: "In three months, my goal is to have completed the assertiveness training course at the YWCA, to speak to at least one person per day in an assertive manner, to maintain eye contact whenever I speak to my husband, and to be taking voice lessons so I can project my voice more forcefully."

2. Names of people outside therapy who will be an ongoing support system.

Example: Suzy Smith, Pastor Jones, my brother Sam, Mary at work.

3. A written assessment of areas of vulnerability can help a person determine how he can avoid falling into old behavior patterns and how he can see the warning signs of a possible relapse early.

Example: "My signs of burnout: constipation for more than three days, skipping my daily jogging routine, craving sweets, forgetting to put gas in the car, leaving things behind, leaving dishes more than twenty-four hours, crabbing at the kids over picky things, forgetting to do my 12 Steps workbook, overdrawing the checking account, leaving the lawn mower out in the rain."

By being aware of danger signals, couples can get their lives back in balance.[6]

4. A written procedure to follow when "slipping" back into old "crazy" behavior.

Example: "When I relapse into old patterns I will: (a) promptly admit my fault to God and at least one other person (Step 5); (b) review in my mind or in my journal what "triggers" I ignored which set me up for this relapse. I will correct any imbalances in my life ASAP; (c) assertively communicate my feelings about any injustice or hurt done to me, without using old negative behavior patterns (I will practice ahead of time what I need to say); (d) If it is not safe for me to communicate my feelings, I will get help from an outside third party. I will seek to protect myself in an adult, mature manner.

Once they have developed an "after-therapy plan," the

misogynist and his wife are encouraged to finish this cycle of their 12 Step Program (Steps 10–12) and begin to go two to four weeks between appointments. At appointment times, the therapist should encourage them to reach out to others and to continue taking care of themselves. Sometimes at this point one or both may experience a setback. This should be viewed as a test of their relapse plan, conducted while still in the safety of the therapeutic relationship. The normal grieving process regarding termination of therapy will also occur as they begin to disengage from the therapist. I encourage individuals to continue for at least one year, if not permanently, in some support group (such as Al-Anon; Codependency Support, "Women Who Love Too Much"). Other community support services may also be necessary, particularly if the couple has decided to divorce. (Usually one or both partners will ask for support separately during the divorce crisis period. The therapist needs to know what support to offer personally and when to refer out.)

10

WHAT CAN THE CHRISTIAN COMMUNITY DO?

BREAKING THE CODE OF SILENCE

The primary thing that the Christian community can do to change the misogynistic system is to break the silence about it. As Christians we must educate ourselves, becoming aware of what a misogynistic relationship looks like. We must examine our own views of issues about sexism, abuse, and male-female relationships.

The Christian community must be educated regarding these issues. We will begin to see change only by talking about sexism and abuse, calling abuse what it is, and challenging people to examine their own relationships. We must create what Sweeten calls a "therapeutic community," where broken people feel safe in being honest about what is going on at home.[1] Misogyny is not the only hidden problem in the Christian family; incest, drug or alcohol dependence, sexual addiction, gambling problems, compulsive spending, eating disorders, and child abuse often go on undetected. Beginning to talk about one dysfunction usually frees people to talk about others.

We must encourage men and women who are recovering from an abusive marriage to speak up. A lay testimony regarding a recovered marriage has tremendous power and benefits many. Hearing peers tell their story is the basis of all the recovery programs such as AA, OA, Al-Anon, and ACA.

We need to provide safe avenues for abused women to seek confidential Christian help. Christian women are reluctant to seek help from "secular" groups like Women Helping Women because they fear an anti-Christian bias. These fears are not without some reason. Although well-meaning, many groups run by non-Christians do not provide the necessary emotional support for Christian women. The staff does not understand their concern with obedience to Scripture or aversion to divorce as the automatic solution. Yet a fear of judgment or of gossip keeps many Christian women from seeking help, even from their pastors. By publicizing the issues of abuse and misogyny, we give these women permission to address them. For many, the first step toward health begins when they read Susan Forward's *Men Who Hate Women—and the Women Who Love Them* or when they listen to taped lectures on the topic, presented or provided by their churches. This has been done with my lectures and tapes on *Male and Female Relationships: Discovering Unhealthy Patterns* and *When Love Hurts: Codependency and Interpersonal Relationships*. Support groups, shelters, and safe houses are also ways Christians can begin to break the silence surrounding misogyny in marriage.

CHANGE THE SEXIST CLIMATE

Along with creating a "therapeutic community" where people feel free to share their problems, we also need to eliminate sexism. Although some churches still believe that women cannot be ordained, they can encourage a shift in the emotional climate toward deeper respect for women. Teaching the Christian community to honor one another in Christ, on the basis of our unity in Him, is a beginning. Paul instructs us that in Christ "there is neither . . . male nor female, for you are all one in Christ Jesus. If you belong to Christ, then you are Abraham's seed, and heirs according to the promise" (Gal. 3:28–29). One way of changing the system is holding men accountable regarding their attitudes and actions toward women. It also helps to discuss the fact that we are all prejudiced in some area.

Another way is to encourage church boards, committees, Bible studies, and youth groups to examine their rationale for doing things in relation to the issue of sexism. Helping women to become more self-respecting and assertive will promote more openness. Often those most vocally opposed to change regarding sexism are women who are afraid of change and of losing their martyr's role in society. Some women have lived with abuse and sexism for so long that they are not even aware of it. Discussion groups, retreats, and seminars about the role of women in the church can help raise awareness regarding these problems.

EMOTIONAL EDUCATION FOR MEN

Men in our culture have been undereducated in the area of emotions and emotional life. Men are often totally unaware of their deepest feelings, needs, fears, and anxieties. Taught to regard these as weaknesses, they have learned from earliest childhood to deny them. Some men are vaguely aware of their pain, but do not know how to verbalize it. For others, anger is the only emotion they feel comfortable with, so they overuse it in their intimate relationships. Sexism stereotypes both men and women; these stereotypes need to be shattered. Traditional masculinity restricts men to a limited range of emotional responses; anger is the most common. Repeated incidents of mislabeled and misidentified feelings can push men toward violence. Men need to be taught a wide range of emotional options. The misogynist needs to understand that his problem is not his wife but his own restricted emotional experience and his deep unconscious fear of abandonment. Teaching men to let go of the stereotyped roles from our society ("Tough Guy," "Superman," "The Lone Ranger," "Give 'em Hell Harry," "J. R. Ewing") frees them to find more balanced patterns of relating to self and to women.

PROVIDE SUPPORT SYSTEMS

Women and men, individually or as couples, who go into recovery need support. The church can be and should be one of the groups providing such support.

Men whose marriages have failed need grace and forgiveness. They need skills to begin again. They need peer support and encouragement. Models are necessary to show these men that they can change. (This statement assumes that in losing their marriages, they recognized their misogyny and began to recover.)

Men who are still in denial need to be challenged. Changing the climate is one way to accomplish the goals of breaking down "denial," yet these men also need support. Change is never easy; it helps to have others around who are a

162

little ahead of them—and a little behind—so they can gauge their progress. Therapy groups for codependent women have sprung up everywhere. There are few groups for misogynistic men, partly because few misogynists recognize their need for help. Therapists must become trained and ready to start helping these men. As we begin to teach and train on this topic, men will respond little by little. When I began teaching on misogyny in 1986, few men responded favorably. Now, a *small* number of men are beginning to respond and ask for help. Reaching out to them is a risky business because of the depth of their denial, but it is gratifying when genuine change does occur.

Women who leave their marriages need help in certain areas. Many have never balanced a checkbook. Most have never purchased any major appliances, bought insurance, or taken out a loan. Usually they have only limited work experience. Even when they worked, it was before marriage or in a part-time capacity at low pay. Most of these women are undereducated for competition in today's marketplace. If there are children, being a working mom is often a terrible burden. Such women feel like second-class citizens at church because they are not fulfilling the role of full-time home-maker. These women may need support in money manage-ment, career development, job training, legal issues, assertive-ness training, single parenting, stress management, and psychological counseling. Dealing with their guilt, shame, and fear will be high on the priority list.

Other women will stay in their marriage even though the husband only slightly changes. They find that they can manage with that small change in the system. Although many would prefer a healthier marriage, they are willing to accept what they have. In essence they have decided to grow within (or around) the relationship because the change in the relationship has enabled them to cope better and to safeguard their mental and physical health. These women also need the reassurance and support of the Christian community. Their situation is not ideal, and we need to be sensitive to their struggles.

CAUTIONS FOR THERAPISTS

Counseling couples is always demanding; working with misogynistic relationships is even more so. It requires that the therapist be aware of their own personal issues regarding abuse and misogyny. I have found that many therapists automatically fault the woman and assume that the woman is "castrating" or "hysterical." Such therapists are easily conned by the husband's debonair manner and verbal skills. I am aware of two cases in which a misogynist, through charm and manipulation, deceived court-appointed psychologists and/or psychiatrists and persuaded them to grant him custody of the minor children. In both cases the man had been abusive to the woman; and in one case he had sexually abused the couple's young daughter.

Countertransference is an issue here. If a male therapist is unaware of his own feelings surrounding abuse and misogyny, he will find it difficult to spot them in others. Female therapists can literally be seduced by the misogynist's charm, wit, intelligence, and persuasive manner. He comes across as the ideal man—loving, charming, kind, and humorous— until you start poking below the surface. When a therapist uncovers the misogynist's flaws, feelings, and role in the relationship, things begin to look different. It is crucial to be aware of the typical "con" used by these men. Reading Forward's book is perhaps the easiest way to understand this issue. Female therapists need to be aware that their own experiences with abuse from men may also interfere with their ability to objectively see the woman's role in the problem. Codependent male and female therapists must be sure to carefully watch their own recovery in order to help such a couple.

CONCLUSION

In this book we have examined misogyny, a destructive marital pattern based on hate for women, fear, and unresolved dependency needs. We have noted the contribution of both women and men to this lifestyle pattern. We have confronted key factors within the Christian community that exacerbate it. The task of change is formidable: individuals, couples, families, churches—all levels of society—must change. The challenge for each of us is to examine and then make improvements within our own lives so that we truly model the skills and lifestyle necessary for changes to occur in the broader networks of our relationships, churches, and society. May we possess the personal serenity needed to do so.

THE SERENITY PRAYER

God, grant me the serenity
    to accept the things I cannot change,
the courage to change the things I can,
    and the wisdom to know the difference.
Living one day at a time;
    enjoying one moment at a time;
accepting hardship as a pathway to peace;
    taking, as Jesus did,
this sinful world as it is,
    not as I would have it;

trusting that You will make all things right
 if I surrender to your will;
so that I may be reasonably happy in this life
 and supremely happy with You forever in the next.
        Reinhold Neibuhr

APPENDIX A

THE TWELVE STEPS

This version of the Twelve Steps of Alcoholics Anonymous is reprinted with permission from *The Twelve Steps - A Spiritual Journey* (San Diego: Recovery Publications, 1988).

Step One

We admitted we were powerless over our separation from God—that our lives had become unmanageable.

> *I know nothing good lives in me, that is, in my sinful nature. For I have the desire to do what is good, but I cannot carry it out* (Romans 7:18).

Step Two

Came to believe that a power greater than ourselves could restore us to sanity.

> *For it is God who works in you to will and to act according to his good purposes* (Philippians 2:13).

Step Three

Made a decision to turn our will and our lives over to the care of God *as we understood Him.*

Therefore I urge you, brothers, in view of God's mercy, to offer your bodies as living sacrifices, holy and pleasing to God—which is your spiritual worship (Romans 12:1).

Step Four

Made a searching and fearless moral inventory of ourselves.

Let us examine our ways and test them, and let us return to the Lord (Lamentations 3:40).

Step Five

Admitted to God, to ourselves, and to another human being the exact nature of our wrongs.

Therefore confess your sins to each other and pray for each other so that you may be healed (James 5:15a).

Step Six

Were entirely ready to have God remove all these defects of character.

Humble yourselves before the Lord, and he will lift you up (James 4:10).

Step Seven

Humbly asked Him to remove our shortcomings.

If we confess our sins, he is faithful and just and will forgive us our sins and purify us from all unrighteousness (1 John 1:9).

Step Eight

Made a list of all persons we had harmed, and became willing to make amends to them all.

> *Do to others as you would have them do to you* (Luke 6:31).

Step Nine

Made direct amends to such people wherever possible, except when to do so would injure them or others.

> *Therefore, if you are offering your gift at the altar and there remember that your brother has something against you, leave your gift there in front of the altar. First go and be reconciled to your brother; then come and offer your gift* (Matthew 5:23–24).

Step Ten

Continued to take personal inventory and when we were wrong promptly admitted it.

> *So, if you think you are standing firm, be careful that you don't fall* (1 Corinthians 10:12).

Step Eleven

Sought through prayer and meditation to improve our conscious contact with God *as we understood Him,* praying only for knowledge of His will for us and the power to carry that out.

> *Let the word of Christ dwell in you richly* (Colossians 3:16a).

Step Twelve

Having had a spiritual awakening as the result of these steps, we tried to carry this message to alcoholics, and to practice these principles in all our affairs.

Brothers, if someone is caught in a sin, you who are spiritual should restore him gently. But watch yourself, or you also may be tempted (Galatians 6:1).

APPENDIX B

COUNSELING RESOURCES

The following organizations provide counseling assistance, treatment, and training programs. Some maintain directories of Christian Psychologists and mental health professionals in various geographical areas of the country.

The Christian Comprehensive Care Corporation offers quality inpatient hospital treatment and outpatient counseling programs through their Life Way counseling programs. Specializes in psychiatric, psychological codependency and substance abuse treatment. Has a syndicated radio show *The Life Way Program.*

> Christian Comprehensive Care Corporation
> 4015 Executive Park Drive, Suite 305
> Cincinnati, Ohio 45241
> 1-800-334-8973
> (513) 769-4600

The Christian Association of Psychological Studies is a membership organization of Christian psychologists, counselors, and social workers. They maintain a directory of

Christian mental health professionals in the United States and Canada. Their directory can be obtained for $10.00.

Christian Association of Psychological Studies (CAPS)
Post Office Box 628
Blue Jay, California 92317
(714)-337-5117

Equipping Ministries International offers many training courses in interpersonal skills, lay counseling, and emotional education for lay and professional counselors, clergy, and church leaders. Purpose of training materials is to equip the church to become a therapeutic community. Offers a consistent schedule of training seminars and has outstanding training materials in printed, audio, and video tape format.

Equipping Ministries International, Suite 309
4015 Executive Park Drive
Cincinnati, Ohio 45241
(513) 769-5353

Focus On The Family has a nationally syndicated radio program, publishes a monthly magazine.

Focus On The Family (Dr. James Dobson)
Counseling Department
801 Corporate Center Drive
Pomona, California 91768
(714)-620-8500

Minirith-Meier Foundation has a nationally syndicated radio program. Provides seminars and a network of mental health-care facilities staffed by Christian health-care professionals.

172

Minirith-Meier Clinic
2100 North Collins Boulevard
Richardson, Texas 75080
1-800-232-9462
1-800-229-4769

Rapha has a national network of Christ-centered health care by credentialed providers. Specializes in psychiatric and substance abuse treatment.

Rapha
8876 Gulf Freeway, Suite 130
Houston, Texas 77017
1-800-227-2657

APPENDIX C

RESOURCE LIST

The following references may be helpful to readers who desire further information on the topic of codependency and misogyny. Dr. Rinck does not necessarily agree with or endorse all viewpoints espoused by these authors. Not all authors listed here represent a Christian evangelical world-view in their discussion of codependency and related topics; however, their works present useful information that can be profitably read by the discerning reader.

Inner Healing and Spiritual Development

Foster, Richard. *Celebration of Discipline,* New York: Harper and Row, 1978.

Kiersey, David and Marilyn Bates. *Please Understand Me,* Del Mar, California: Prometheus Nemesis Books, 1978.

Linn, Matthew and Dennis. *Healing Life's Hurts,* New York: Paulist Press, 1978.

Payne, Leanne. *The Broken Image: Restoring Personal Wholeness Through Healing Prayer,* Westchester, Ill.: Crossway Books, 1981.

Payne, Leanne. *Crisis in Masculinity,* Westchester, Ill.: Crossway Books, 1985.

Rubin, Theodore Isaac. *The Angry Book,* New York: Macmillan Publishing, 1969.

Sandford, J. A. *Dreams and Healing,* New York: Paulist Press, 1978.

Sandford, John and Paula. *Transformation of the Inner Man,* South Plainfield, N.J.: Bridge Publishing Company, 1982.

Smedes, Lewis B. *Forgive and Forget: Healing the Hurts That We Don't Deserve,* New York: Pocket Books, 1984.

Male and Female Relationships

Beattie, Melody. *Codependent No More,* Center City, Minn.: Hazelden, 1987.

Bessell, Howard. *The Love Test,* New York: Wm. Morrow and Company, 1984.

Black, Claudia. *It'll Never Happen to Me,* Denver: M.A.C. Printing and Publications, 1981.

Carnes, Patrick. *Out of the Shadows,* Minneapolis: Comp Care, 1983.

Carter, Steven. *Men Who Can't Love,* New York: M. Evans & Company, 1987.

Cowan, Connell and Melvyn Kinder. *Smart Women: Foolish Choices,* New York: Clarkson and Potter, Inc.. 1985.

Cruise, Sharon W. *Choice Making,* Pompano Beach: Health Communications, 1985.

Forward, Susan. *Men Who Hate Women and the Women Who Love Them,* New York: Bantam Books, 1986.

Kiley, Dan. *The Peter Pan Syndrome,* New York: Avon Books 1983.

Kiley, Dan. *The Wendy Dilemma,* New York: Arbor House, 1984.

Leonard, Linda Schierse. *The Wounded Woman: Healing the Father-Daughter Relationship,* Boston: Shambula, 1982.

Sandford, J. A. *Invisible Partners,* New York: Paulist Press, 1980.

Shainess, Natalie. *Sweet Suffering: Woman as Victim,* New York: Bobbs-Merrill Company, 1984.

Strom, Kay Marshall. *In the Name of Submission: A Painful Look at Wife Battering,* Portland, Ore.: Multnomah Press, 1986.

Codependency and Recovery

Larsen, Earnie. *Stage II Relationships: Love Beyond Addiction,* San Francisco: Harper and Row, 1987.

Lenters, William. *The Freedom We Crave: Addiction—The Human Condition,* Grand Rapids, Mich.: Wm. Eerdmans Co., 1985.

Middleton-Moz, Jane and Lorie Dwinell. *After the Tears: Reclaiming the Personal Losses of Childhood,* Pompano Beach: Health Communications, 1986.

Rinck, Margaret J. *Can Christians Love Too Much?: Breaking the Cycle of Codependency,* Grand Rapids: Zondervan, 1989.

Rinck, Margaret J. *When Love Hurts: Codependency and Interpersonal Relationships,* Cincinnati: Act Resources, 1988.

Schneider, Jennifer P. *Back From Betrayal: Recovering From His Affairs,* Center City, Minn.: Hazelden Educational Materials, 1988.

Wilson-Schaef, Anne. *Codependence: Misunderstood—Mistreated,* New York: Harper and Row, 1986.

Educational Materials

Woititz, Janet. *Adult Children of Alcoholics,* Hollywood: Health Communications, 1983.

Woititz, Janet. *Home Away From Home: The Art of Self-Sabotage,* Pompano Beach: Health Communications, 1987.

Woititz, Janet. *Struggle for Intimacy,* Pompano Beach: Health Communications, 1985.

Workbooks

Black, Claudia. *Repeat After Me,* Denver: M.A.C. Printing and Publications, 1985.

Carnes, Patrick. *A Gentle Way Through the 12 Steps,* Minneapolis: Comp Care Publications, 1989.

God Help Me Stop. Anonymous (P.O. Box 27364, San Diego, CA 92128).

The Twelve Steps: A Spiritual Journey (Anon. Recovery Publications, 1201 Knoxville Street, San Diego, CA 92110).

Books to Help You Cope

Brilles, Judith. *Dollars and Sense of Divorce,* New York: Master Media Ltd., 1988.

Brilles, Judith. *Faith and Savvy Too,* New York: Master Media Ltd., 1988.

Brilles, Judith. *Woman to Woman: From Sabotage to Support,* Far Hills, N.J., 1987.

Drews, Toby Rice. *Getting Them Sober* (vols. 1–3), South Plainfield, N.J.: Bridge Publishing, 1980, 1983, 1986.

Hart, Archibald. *Adrenalin and Stress,* Waco, Tex.: Word Books, 1986.

APPENDIX C

Books on Shared Leadership and Mutual Submission in Marriage

Bilezikian, Gilbert. *Beyond Sex Roles: What the Bible Says About a Woman's Place in Church and Family,* Grand Rapids: Baker Book House, 1989.

Gundry, Patricia. *Heirs Together: Mutual Submission in Marriage,* Grand Rapids: Zondervan, 1980.

Hull, Gretchen Gaebelien. *Equal to Serve: Women and Men in the Church and Home,* Old Tappan, N.J.: Fleming Revell, 1987.

Martin, Faith. *Call Me Blessed: The Emerging Christian Woman,* Grand Rapids: Eerdmans, 1988.

Olthius, James H. *I Pledge You My Troth: A Christian View of Marriage, Family, Friendship,* New York: Harper and Row, 1975.

APPENDIX D

LIFE SEMINARS

In my books I often refer to the importance of the church as a therapeutic community. Equipping Ministries International is one of the few organizations of which I am aware that fundamentally integrates the Christian worldview with psychology and educational resources so as to provide a systematic training program to church leaders for renewal in the local church. Renewal in the local church is a key issue for the Christian community as we attempt to address institutional issues of codependency and misogyny.

In addition to their workshops and programs in book, audio cassette, and video tape cassette form, Life Seminars offers regular training workshops.

Goal: Help pastors and other church leaders to be successful in ministry.

Objective: To make the church of Jesus Christ into a caring, healing, growth community.

Means: To enable pastors and other leaders to effectively and practically know how to "equip their members so that they are actually doing the work of ministry."

Workshops and available materials include:

Apples of Gold I—Developing the Fruit of the Spirit: A foundational course in interpersonal skills training of empathy, warmth, and respect in relationships.

Apples of Gold II—Speaking the Truth in Love: How to confront in love; resist inappropriate behavior; deal with angry people; manage conflict, and move others to positive steps.

Rational Christian Thinking—Renewing the Mind: How to deal with anxiety-provoking thoughts, depression, compulsions, and fears. Subjects include the importance of mind in Scripture, how to train yourself to think rationally and combat irrational self-talk.

Breaking Free from the Past—Healing Life's Hurts: For mature, well trained people with caring skills and self-awareness. Focuses on mutual confession, forgiveness, and intercessory prayer. Requires as prerequisite all of the above-listed courses plus other requirements.

The Theology of Caring, Equipping Community: Course covers the integration of psychology, theology, and the power of the Holy Spirit. Practical considerations for setting up a lay counseling center.

Growing as a Christian Family: A pilot workshop developed by a family therapist on how the family and the church congregation can be places of healing and growth.

Won by One—Friendship Evangelism: How you can effectively help your friends and family (including children) to discover a personal relationship with Jesus Christ. Based on Dr. Ronald Rand's book of the same title.

Small Groups—Workable Wineskins: Covers many aspects of small group life, focusing upon: ways groups can be used in the church; communicating effectively to build relationships; stages groups go through; various other group dynamics, and some practical how-to's for the functioning and growth of groups.

Training Lay Pastors: Course was designed to provide pastoral care of every member of the church body by calling forth and equipping lay people who have pastoral gifts.

In addition to the above courses, other training and courses are available to train participants to teach the foundational courses in their own local congregations.

For more information about training and courses, write to:

Equipping Ministries International
4015 Executive Park Drive, Suite 309
Cincinnati, Ohio 45241
(513) 769-5353

APPENDIX E

WHAT IS MISOGYNY?

You may photocopy this appendix and Figure I for the purpose of sharing information about misogyny with a prospective counselor.

What is misogyny? The word is unfamiliar to most people. It comes from the Greek words μισογυνια *misein*, meaning to hate, and *gune*, meaning women. Literally, misogyny means the hatred of women. Misogyny entails a pattern of mental and emotional abuse in marital and male/female relationships. While misogynistic behavior can include physical abuse, it is usually much more subtle. Unlike the usual stereotype of men who hate women, such as wife beaters and rapists, the usual misogynistic male primarily uses emotional and mental weapons against his partner.

The partner of the misogynist is usually very bewildered. What happened to the man with whom she fell in love? After the honeymoon has ended, she realizes that she married not Romeo, but Dr. Jekyll and Mr. Hyde.

The fact is that women in misogynistic relationships are constantly dealing with a double-minded man. Her partner at times is charming, adoring, affable, and loving; the next moment he is likely to be controlling, mean-spirited, and cruel. The wife is likely to be so confused by the mixed messages of her relationship that she wonders if she is going crazy. She thinks that because he can behave so lovingly at times, that it *must* be her fault that he is not *always* that way. Women in these dysfunctional relationships are usually very codependent. When they are scapegoated by their spouse as being the cause of the problems in the relations—they tend to accept the blame.

Christian men who hate women (religious misogynists) are in some ways more dangerous and destructive in their behavior than their non-Christian counterparts. Secular misogynists do not have the powerful, additional arsenal of church doctrines, God-talk, and the sanctioning of male authority, which comes with the idea of Christian marriage. Christian women are often taught in the church or at home that they should "submit" to men "no matter what" because men are the "spiritual head" over women.

What is confusing to the woman is the double-sided nature of the man's behavior. He frequently acts one way at home and then presents a different face to the outside world. When he is at church or work, he is witty, kind, considerate. Often his wife finds that her pastor and friends at church do not believe her confessions of abuse because they never see his misogynistic side. This double-life factor keeps the wife and others off balance. She becomes convinced that if she would "just do what he says" or "try harder" or "be more loving" then he would be consistently kind and caring to her.

I have seen cases where psychologists, psychiatrists, and pastors have been totally fooled by the good-looking facade of these men. Misogynists are usually quite bright and quite capable of doing a snowjob to escape detection by a professional therapist. Even when a misogynist is confronted with evidence of his abusive behavior, he may respond by saying, "I know I did that—but it's only because I needed to teach her a lesson. If she would just do as I say, everything would be fine."

Misogynists are unable to empathize with their wives' pain and distress. In fact, the pain of their partner seems to enrage them and feed their hatred. Here are some telltale signs of a misogynistic relationship:

1. The man assumes that it is his "God-given right" to control how his wife lives and behaves. Her needs, thoughts, feelings are not considered.

2. He uses God, the Bible, and church teachings to support his right to "tell her what to do," and demands that she *submit* to his desires, whims, decisions, or plans without question. There is no sense of mutuality or loving consideration. It's always his way, or no way.

3. He believes that a woman's beliefs, opinions, views, feelings, and thoughts are of no real value. He may discredit her opinions in general or specifically because she is a "daughter of Eve and easily deceived." Therefore, her opinions are of little consequence. Or alternatively, he may give lip service to the idea that his wife's opinions count for something, but then discount them one by one because they are not "logical."

4. The woman reports that her husband's behavior at home is strikingly different from his behavior at work or at church. At home everyone "walks on eggs" out of fear of displeasing him or setting him off. When the wife points out the difference between his behavior at home and other places, he is likely to respond, "Oh, quit exaggerating! I'm not like that!"

5. The woman reports that when he is displeased and/or does not get his way, he yells and threatens, or sulks in angry silence. Yet the next day he acts as if "nothing"

had happened, and is charming and sweet. No one can predict when he is going to switch from nice to nasty.

6. The woman finds that in her relationship with him, no matter how much she may try to improve, change, "grow in the Word," etc., she still feels inadequate, guilty, and somehow off-balance. She never knows what is going to set him off next, and no matter how much she prays, he never changes. She almost feels as if she must be "crazy," and she is sure it is her fault. Even when other relationships at work or school give her positive feedback and encouragement, she loses all her confidence and self-esteem when she returns home. No matter what she does to change and adapt to his demands, it is never enough. His demands always change and become unreasonable.

7. The husband remains blind to any fault or cruelty on his part. When anything goes wrong in the home or in the marital relationship, the problem is always *the woman*. If she would just be "more submissive" or "be filled with the Spirit" or "obey me like a good Christian wife," everything would be fine. He actually sees himself as virtuous for "putting up" with a woman like her. On the other hand, he can become unreasonably jealous if other people, particularly men, pay too much attention to his wife. Thus, the wife no longer feels free to associate with certain friends, groups, or family members because of her need to keep him happy. Even though these activities or people are important to her, she prefers avoiding them so that she can "keep the peace."

If you see a relationship that has most of these characteristics, you are dealing with a misogynist. If as a pastor or counselor, you meet a woman who comes in for counseling

and she describes a relationship that sounds like this, there is
misogyny involved.

NOTES

INTRODUCTION

[1] *The American Heritage Dictionary, Second College Edition* (Boston: Houghton Mifflin, 1985), 803.
[2] Susan Forward, *Men Who Hate Women and the Women Who Love Them* (New York: Bantam Books, 1986), 6–8.
[3] Ibid., 6–8.
[4] Ibid., 8.
[5] Ibid., 10.

1—THE DILEMMA OF SUBMISSION AND ABUSE

[1] Kay Marshall Strom, *In the Name of Submission: A Painful Look at Wife Battering* (Portland, Ore.: Multnomah, 1986), 52.
[2] M. A. Straus, R. H. Gelles, and S. K. Steinmetz, *Behind Closed Doors* (New York: Doubleday Books, 1981), 32.
[3] Ibid., 136–39.

2—THE MISOGYNIST

[1] *Diagnostic and Statistical Manual of Mental Disorders* DSM III-R (Washington, D.C.: American Psychiatric Association, 1987), 349.
[2] Susan Forward, *Men Who Hate Women and the Women Who Love Them* (New York: Bantam Books, 1986), 58–70.
[3] Ibid., 70–76.
[4] Ibid., 76–78.
[5] Ibid., 20.

3—WOMEN WHO MARRY MISOGYNISTS

[1] Robin Norwood, *Women Who Love Too Much* (Los Angeles: Jeremy P. Tarcher, 1985).

[2] Melody Beattie, *Codependent No More* (Center City, Minn.: Hazelden, 1987), 85–86.

[3] Judith Viorst, *Necessary Losses* (New York: Simon and Schuster, 1986), 76–80.

[4] Beattie, *Codependent No More*, 76–80.

4—ISSUES IN THE CHRISTIAN MARRIAGE

[1] Robert M. Goldenson, ed., *Longman Dictionary of Psychology and Psychiatry* (New York: Longman, 1984), 674.

[2] Ibid.

[3] Dennis Sloat, *The Dangers of Growing Up in a Christian Home* (New York: Nelson, 1986), 99; John Geier and Dorothy E. Downey, *The Inspirational Pattern*, vol. 6, *Library of Classical Profile Patterns* (Minneapolis: Performance Systems International, 1979), 16–17, 19–20.

[4] Sloat, *The Dangers of Growing Up*, 99.

[5] Geier and Downey, *The Inspirational Pattern*, 16–17, 19–20.

[6] Paul Tournier, *The Strong and the Weak*, E. Hudson, trans. (Philadelphia: Westminster, 1979), 20–23.

[7] Esther Lee Olson and K. Petersen, *No Place to Hide: Wife Abuse—Anatomy of a Private Crime* (Wheaton: Tyndale House, 1985), 132.

5—ROOT PROBLEMS: SHAME AND FEAR OF ABANDONMENT

[1] Lowell L. Noble, *Naked and Not Ashamed* (Jackson, Mich.: Jackson Printing, 1975), 20–23.

[2] Ruth Benedict, *The Chrysanthemum and the Sword* (Boston: Houghton Mifflin, 1946), passim.

[3] Noble, *Naked and Not Ashamed*, 20–23.

[4] Margaret Josephson Rinck, *Can Christians Love Too Much? Breaking the Cycle of Codependency* (Grand Rapids: Zondervan, 1989).

[5] John Bradshaw, *Healing the Shame That Binds You* (Deerfield Beach, Fla.: Health Communications, 1988), 88–95.

7—THE WOMAN IN THERAPY AND TREATMENT

[1] Robert R. Corkhuff, *Helping and Human Relations,* vols. 1, 2 (New York: Holt, Rinehart and Winston, 1969), passim.

[2] George M. Gazda, *Human Relations Development: A Manual for Educators* (Boston: Allyn and Bacon, 1973), passim.

[3] Gary Ray Sweeten, *Training Lay People in the Local Church,* Doctoral Dissertation, University of Cincinnati, Dissertation Abstracts International, 1975, passim; Gary Ray Sweeten, *The Theology of an Equipping and Caring Community* (Cincinnati: Christian Information Committee, 1981), passim.

[4] Patrick Carnes, *Counseling the Sexual Addict,* Symposium presented at the Institute of Behavioral Medicine, Golden Valley, Minn., September 1988.

[5] Ibid.

[6] Ibid.

[7] Robin Norwood, *Women Who Love Too Much* (Los Angeles: Jeremy P. Tarcher, 1985), passim.

[8] Maxie Maultsby, *Help Yourself to Happiness Through Rational Self-Counseling* (New York: Institute for Rational Living, 1975), 7–8, 27–43.

[9] Judith Viorst, *Necessary Losses* (New York: Simon and Schuster, 1986), passim.

[10] M. Bowen, *Family Therapy in Clinical Practice* (New York: Jason Aronson, 1978), passim.

[11] M. McGoldrick and R. Gerson, *Genograms in Family Assessment* (New York: Norton, 1985), passim.

[12] Patrick Carnes, *A Gentle Way Through the 12 Steps* (Minneapolis: Comp Care, 1988).

[13] Natalie Shainess, *Sweet Suffering: Woman as Victim* (New York: Bobbs-Merrill Company, 1984), 38–65.

[14] Norwood, *Women Who Love Too Much* (Los Angeles: Jeremy P. Tarcher, 1985).

[15] Viorst, *Necessary Losses,* 79–80.

8—THE MISOGYNIST IN THERAPY AND TREATMENT

[1] Susan Forward, *Men Who Hate Women and the Women Who Love Them* (New York: Bantam Books, 1986), passim.

9—THE STEPS TO RECOVERY

[1] John Bradshaw, *Healing the Shame That Binds You* (Deerfield Beach, Fla.: Health Communications, 1988).

[2] Merle A. Fossum and Marilyn J. Mason, *Facing Shame: Families in Recovery* (New York: Norton, 1986), passim.

[3] Peck, M. Scott, *The Road Less Traveled* (New York: Simon and Schuster, 1986), passim.

[4] Gary Ray Sweeten, *The Theology of an Equipping and Caring Community* (Cincinnati: Christian Information Committee, 1981), passim.

[5] M. Meichenbaum, *Cognitive-Behavior Modification: An Integrative Approach* (New York: Plenum, 1985), passim.

[6] Patrick Carnes, *Counseling the Sexual Addict,* Symposium presented at the Institute of Behavioral Medicine, Golden Valley, Minn., September 1988, passim.

10—WHAT CAN THE CHRISTIAN COMMUNITY DO?

[1] Gary Ray Sweeten, *Training Lay People in the Local Church,* Doctoral Dissertation, University of Cincinnati, Dissertation Abstracts International, 1975, passim.

BIBLIOGRAPHY

Alcoholics Anonymous World Services, Inc. *Alcoholics Anonymous,* 3rd ed., New York, 1976.

American Psychiatric Association. *Diagnostic and Statistical Manual of Mental Disorders,* 3rd rev. ed., Washington, D.C., 1987.

Beattie, Melody. *Codependent No More,* Center City, Minn.: Hazelden, 1987.

Benedict, Ruth. *The Chrysanthemum and the Sword,* Boston: Houghton Mifflin, 1946.

Bowen, M. *Family Therapy in Clinical Practice,* New York: Jason Aronson, 1978.

Bradshaw, John. *Healing the Shame That Binds You,* Deerfield Beach, Fla.: Health Communications, 1988.

Carkhuff, R. R. *Helping and Human Relations,* vols. 1 & 2. New York: Holt, Rinehart and Winston, 1969.

Carnes, Patrick. *Counseling the Sexual Addict* (Symposium presented at the Institute of Behavioral Medicine). Golden Valley, Minn.: September 1988.

Forward, Susan. *Men Who Hate Women and the Women Who Love Them,* New York: Bantam Books, 1986.

Fossum, Merle A. and Marilyn J. Mason. *Facing Shame: Families in Recovery,* New York: Norton, 1986.

Gazda, George M. *Human Relations Development: A Manual for Educators,* Boston: Allyn and Bacon, 1973.

Geier, John G. *Personal Profile System Manual,* Minneapolis: Performance Systems International, 1979 (rev. 1983).

Geier, John G. and Dorothy E. Downey. *The Inspirational Pattern,* vol. 6. *Library of Classical Profile Patterns,* Minneapolis: Performance Systems International, 1979.

Goldenson, Robert M. ed. *Longman Dictionary of Psychology and Psychiatry,* New York: Longman Inc., 1984.

Gondolf, E. W. *Men Who Batter: An Integrated Approach for Stopping Wife Abuse,* Holmes Beach, Fla.: Learning Publications, 1985.

Linn, Matthew and Dennis Linn. *Healing Life's Hurts,* New York: Paulist Press, 1978.

Maultsby, Maxie. *Help Yourself to Happiness Through Rational Self-Counseling,* New York: Institute for Rational Living, 1975.

McGoldrick, M., and R. Gerson. *Genograms in Family Assessment,* New York: Norton, 1985.

Meichenbaum, Michael. *Cognitive-Behavior Modification: An Integrative Approach,* New York: Plenum, 1985.

Noble, Lowell L. *Naked and Not Ashamed,* Jackson, Mich.: Jackson Printing, 1975.

Norwood, Robin. *Women Who Love Too Much,* Los Angeles: Jeremy P. Tarcher, 1985.

Olson, Esther L., and K. Petersen. *No Place to Hide: Wife Abuse—Anatomy of a Private Crime,* Wheaton: Tyndale House, 1985.

Peck, M. Scott. *The Road Less Traveled,* New York: Simon and Schuster, 1986.

Rinck, Margaret J. *Can Christians Love Too Much? Breaking the Cycle of Codependency,* Grand Rapids: Zondervan, 1989.

Rinck, Margaret J. *Male and Female Relationships: Discovering Unhealthy Patterns,* Cincinnati: Act Resources, 1987.

Sandford, John and Paula Sandford. *Restoring the Christian Family,* South Plainfield, N.J.: Bridge Publishing, 1986.

Sandford, John and Paula Sandford. *Transformation of the Inner Man,* South Plainfield, N.J.: Bridge Publishing, 1982.

Shainess, Natalie. *Sweet Suffering: Woman as Victim,* New York: Bobbs-Merrill, 1984.

Sloat, Dennis. *The Dangers of Growing Up in a Christian Home,* New York: Nelson, 1986.

Straus, M. A., R. H. Gelles, and S. K. Steinmetz. *Behind Closed Doors,* New York: Doubleday Books, 1981.

Strom, Kay Marshall. *In the Name of Submission: A Painful Look at Wife Battering,* Portland, Ore.: Multnomah, 1986.

Sweeten, Gary Ray. *Training Lay People in the Local Church,* Doctoral Dissertation, University of Cincinnati: Dissertation Abstracts International, 1975.

Sweeten, Gary Ray. *The Theology of an Equipping and Caring Community,* Cincinnati: Christian Information Committee, 1981.

Sweeten, Gary Ray. *Breaking Free from the Past,* Cincinnati: Cincinnati Information Committee, 1983.

Tournier, Paul. *The Strong and the Weak,* E. Hudson, trans. Philadelphia: Westminster, 1976.

Viorst, Judith. *Necessary Losses,* New York: Simon and Schuster, 1986.

RECOMMENDED CASSETTE TAPES

Dr. Rinck's seminars, workshops, and lectures have been professionally recorded and are available on cassette tape. For a brochure and ordering information on these and other tapes, write to:

ACT RESOURCES
Audio Counseling Training Resources
P.O. Box 24177, Department M
Cincinnati, Ohio 45224

Male and Female Relationships: Discovering Unhealthy Patterns. This ten-cassette series examines the dynamics of interpersonal relationships. Includes discussion of codependency and misogyny in relationships. How do past family patterns affect our present relationships? Particular emphasis is on the study of four unhealthy patterns that occur in Male/Female Relationships: (1) Unequal Balance of Power - Man as Controller/Woman as Victim - Woman as Controller/Man as Victim; (2) Immaturity: Games in Relationships; (3) Love as Addiction: Codependency; (4) Relationship Burnout. The first half of the series deals with the diagnosis and root cause of these patterns. The last half suggests how these patterns may be realigned. Presents guidelines for healthy relationships based on emotional maturity. We recommend this tape series to those who have read Dr. Rinck's books on misogyny and codependency.

Can Christians Love Too Much? Breaking the Cycle of Codependency. Love is a problem for many Christians who confuse nurturing and servanthood with destructive codependent enabling and caretaking behaviors. How does the church itself unwittingly promote codependency? This extremely comprehensive nine-cassette audio series provides an integrated approach to identifying, treating, and recovering from codependency from a Christian perspective. We recommend this tape series to those who have read Dr. Rinck's books on misogyny and codependency.

When Love Hurts: Codependency and Interpersonal Relationships. A four-cassette series that was originally part of in-service training for lay church counselors. It deals comprehensively with the subject of codependency. Dr. Rinck integrates information from a wide spectrum of the codependency literature. Topics include: (1) What is codependency? How is it expressed in relationships? Who is vulnerable to the codependency syndrome? (2) Characteristics of codependency relationships. How do I know if I am in such a relationship? What are the signs of an addictive relationship? (3) Characteristics of codependent people. What personality and behavioral traits do codependent people exhibit? How is codependency perpetuated in the relationship? (4) Breaking the cycle of codependency. Understanding the spiritual dynamics of codependency. Freedom from codependency.

Christian Men Who Hate Women Dr. Rinck describes the dynamics of misogynistic relationships. What are the characteristics of abusive relationships? What are the characteristics of the Christian misogynist? What kind of a woman marries a misogynist? What background factors produce a misogynistic relationship? What are the issues for the Christian community? From Dr. Rinck's 90-minute workshop on misogyny presented at the International Congress on Christian Counseling.

About Margaret Josephson Rinck:

Margaret Josephson Rinck was born in Bridgeport, Connecticut, and grew up in nearby Trumbull. She is the eldest of six children (five girls and one boy). Her parents are devoted Christians who reared all their children to know the Lord through their own Christian commitment and involvement in missions, which influenced Margaret to become involved in Christian vocations and ministry.

She graduated summa cum laude with a bachelor's degree in psychology from Gordon College in Wenham, Massachusetts. She received the Master of Religious Education (M.R.E.) from Gordon-Conwell Theological Seminary. Her doctoral degree in counseling (Ed.D.) was awarded at the University of Cincinnati in 1979. Dr. Rinck has been active in church discipleship and counseling ministries in various local churches. She was a staff associate in the college ministry at Park Street Congregational Church in Boston. She served as a missions consultant, a counselor, and staff associate at College Hill Presbyterian Church in Cincinnati, Ohio.

Dr. Rinck is a clinical psychologist in private practice in Cincinnati, Ohio. She works with her husband, John, who manages their psychology practice and Act Resources, a self-publishing venture. She is the author of various curriculum, books, and tape series on interpersonal relationships, marriage, codependency, emotional health, spirituality, and skills training. She is sought after as a speaker for retreats, conferences, and adult Sunday school classes. She periodically conducts therapy groups for Adult Children of Alcoholics and "Women Who Love Too Much." She is the author of *Can Christians Love Too Much?*, published by Zondervan in the fall of 1989.

To the Reader:

We welcome your thoughts, feelings, and reactions to the material presented in *Christian Men Who Hate Women: Healing Hurting Relationships* and in *Can Christians Love Too Much?: Breaking the Cycle of Codependency.*

If you would like to share your personal story, comments, or suggestions regarding either of these two books, we would certainly value hearing from you. You can write to Dr. Rinck:

> ACT Resources
> Audio Counseling Training Resources
> P. O. Box 24177
> Cincinnati, Ohio 45224

We cannot promise that Dr. Rinck will be able to respond to all letters that she receives but she will thoughtfully read every one. May God bless you in your personal journey toward wholeness!